Real-Life Writing & Study Skills

Reproducible Activity Sheets for Grades 4-6

Troll Associates

Troll Teacher Time Savers provide a quick source of self-contained lessons and practice material, designed to be used as full-scale lessons or to make productive use of those precious extra minutes that sometimes turn up in the day's schedule.

Troll Teacher Time Savers can help you to prepare a made-to-order program for your students. Select the sequence of Time Savers that will meet your students' needs, and make as many photocopies of each page as you require. Since Time Savers include progressive levels of complexity and difficulty in each book, it is possible to individualize instruction, matching the needs of each student.

Those who need extra practice and reinforcement for catching up in their skills can benefit from Troll Teacher Time Savers, while other students can use Time Savers for enrichment or as a refresher for skills in which they haven't had recent practice. Time Savers can also be used to diagnose a student's knowledge and skills level, in order to see where extra practice is needed.

Time Savers can be used as homework assignments, classroom or small-group activities, shared learning with partners, or practice for standardized testing.

See "Answer Key & Skills Index" to find the specific skill featured in each activity.

Pages 1-22 review the uses of the dictionary, including alphabetizing, guide words, pronunciation symbols, and parts of speech.

Pages 23-32 focus on maps, charts, and graphs—how to read and interpret them.

Pages 33-52 deal with reference works found in libraries, including almanacs, encyclopedias, and newspapers, and how to use them for research purposes.

Pages 53-61 are exercises in real-life writing that include directions, letters, reports, and forms.

Pages 62-70 concentrate on making sense of everyday reference material, such as newspaper ads, telephone listings, restaurant menus, timetables, and schedules.

Pages 71 to 74 are review exercises, incorporating all of the above skills.

ANSWER KEY & SKILLS INDEX

Page 1, **Super Circus Mystery:** Circus Elephants Found Near Old Railroad Station Tasting Watermelons Yesterday. **(alphabetizing, first letter)**

Page 2, **Priscilla's Peculiar Pet:** 1-baboon; 2-bear; 3-buffalo; 4-mink; 5-mongoose; 6-muskrat; 7-setter; 8-shark; 9-skunk; orang-utan. **(alphabetizing, first and second letter)**

Page 3, **Franklin Stein, Monster Maker:** 1-badger teeth; 2-bamboo shoots; 3-banana peels; 4-mackintosh; 5-magic beans; 6-mahogany roots; 7-mallard feathers; 8-mammoth lips; 9-mantis wings; 10-mare's knees; 11-mashed beetle feet; 12-mayonnaise; the headlines. **(alphabetizing, first, second, third letters)**

Page 4, **Look at the Lexicon!:** 1-c; 2-c; 3-noun; 4-lexicons or lexica; 5-c; 6-b; 7-a; 8-c. **(dictionary)**

Page 5, **Help the Ground Hog:** slumber-221; squint-223; shortsighted-219; squirrel-223; sunshine-225; sleep-221; severe-212; superstition-225; shade-212; sunlight-225; springtime-223; shelter-219; shadow-212. **(guide words)**

Page 6, **The Entry Sentry:** W-23rd letter; vegetable-plant grown for food; Washington, George-first president; un-not; U.S.A.-America; Washington-state or capital of U.S.; -ward-suffix; wouldn't-contraction. **(entry)**

Page 7, **Say What?:**
(pronunciation)

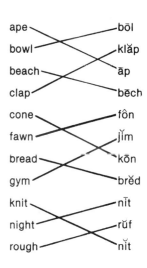

Page 41, **Make a Note of It:** Answers will vary. **(note taking)**

Page 42, **Dora's Dogs:** I-Sal; A-collie; B-long hair; II-Chief; A-dalmatian; B-short hair; III-Dale; A-airedale; B-medium hair. **(outlining)**

Page 43, **The Great Library Mystery:** top row, l to r-F HAY; F HEI; F MIL; bottom, l to r-523B; 551M; 596M; 597B. **(call numbers)**

Page 44, **Paula's Puzzling Problem:** 1-900 to 999; 2-600 to 699; 3-300 to 399; 4-700 to 799; 5-100 to 199; 6-800 to 899; 7-500 to 599; 8-400 to 499; 9-200 to 299; 10-000 to 099. **(Dewey decimal system)**

Page 45, **Library Crossword:** 1-index; 2-glossary; 3-title; 4-author; 5-title page; 6-cover; 7-text; 8-appendix; 9-illustrator; 10-table of contents; 11-bibliography; 12-publisher; 13-preface; 14-call number; 15-spine. **(parts of a book)**

Page 46, **Clumsy Clarence:** fiction-MacGregor, Slobodkin, Twain, Verne, Wells, Williams; nonfiction-Rancan, Eastman, Ford, Coy, Clements, Paige. **(fiction & nonfiction)**

Page 47, **Who's Who?:** A, B, A, B, B, B, B; Barton, John, Keller, Magellan, Sacajawea, Tubman, Zabriskie. **(biography/autobiography)**

Page 48, **For Your Information:** 1-dictionary; 2-encyclopedia; 3-atlas; 4-geographical dictionary; 5-almanac; 6-biographical dictionary; 7-Readers' Guide; 8-thesaurus. **(reference)**

Page 49, **Time to Talk:** Answers will vary. **(interviewing)**

Page 50, **Research an Animal:** Answers will vary. **(research)**

Page 51, **Extra! Extra!:** Answers will vary. **(research)**

Page 52, **Check the Facts:** Mts. cover 1/5 of land; Mt. Everest is in Asia; Sir Edmund Hillary was from New Zealand; date of climb was 1953. **(research)**

Page 53, **Letter to the Editor:** Answers will vary. **(opinion writing)**

Page 54, **How Do I Get There?:** 1-left on Tulip St., right on Third St., left on Maple Ct.; 2-cross B'way to Second St., make right on Rose St., left on Oak Ave. to Tulip St.; 3-Oak Ave. to Rose St., right to Second St. or left to Third St. **(writing directions)**

Page 55, **The Right Recipe:** Answers will vary. **(writing directions)**

Page 56, **Roving Reporter:** Answers will vary. **(writing news story)**

Page 57, **Write an Ad:** Answers will vary. **(persuasive writing)**

Page 58, **Let's Go to the Movies:** 1-Cinema 3; 2-5; 3-2:15, 9:15; 4-2:30, 5:30, about 3 hrs.; 5-MM longer; 6-12:00; 7-MM. **(reading a schedule)**

Page 59, **Super Skates:** 1-Mon.; 2-Wed., Sat., Sun.; 3-Sun. 9-11:30; 4-Tues. or Thurs. 4-6; 5-roller disco; 6-4:00; 7-3; 8-yes. **(reading a schedule)**

Page 60, **The Great Getaway:** 1-5:00 P.M.; 2-no; 3-7:15 P.M.; 4-1 hr., 55 min.; 5-7:15 A.M.; 6-P.M. **(reading a timetable)**

Page 61, **Find It Fast:** Landry, Lane; Keegan, Keller; Boyd, Bradford; Lindsay, Lipton; King, Klaus; Field-Figaro, Fine, Fimmel; Finn-Fipps; 1-Morgan; 2-Mt. Pleasant Ski Shop; 3-16th St. Drug Store; 4-J. Stiles; 5-J.R. Stiles; 6-John Stiles; 7-Maria Suarez; 8-Ramon Suarez. **(telephone book)**

Page 62, **Goods & Services:** Pete's Pizzas-Restaurants, Restaurants/Restaurants; The Hobby House-Toys Retail, Towing/Trailers; Puppy Palace-Pet Shops, Paving/Pewter; Ray Cook, Lawyers, Lawn/Lawyers; Bergen Drugs-Pharmacies, Pharmacies/Photo; Martha Chang-Dentists, Delivery/Dentists; Barbers-East Side Haircutters, House of Hair, Ken's Barber Shop, Kool Cuts, Super Scissors; Music-Dynamite CD's, Music Madness, Record World, Stereo Surprise, Steve's Stereo Shop. **(telephone book)**

Page 63, **Shopping Shortcuts:** 1-Skate Land; 2-Ice World; 3-Skate World; 4-Magic Roller Rink; 5-Magic Roller Rink; 6-Ice World; 7-Roll-A-Round; 8-Magic Roller Rink; 9-323-1132; 10-p. 322. **(telephone book)**

Page 64, **Emergency! Emergency!:** Answers will vary. **(telephone book)**

Page 65, **It's for You!:** 1-a; 2-a; 3-b; 4-c; 5-a. **(telephone courtesy)**

Page 66, **Keep in Touch:** Answers will vary. **(friendly letters)**

Page 67, **Clearly Stated:** 1-Lucy Rettle; 2-7777 Park Ave., N.Y., N.Y. 10010; 3-June 18, 1993; 4-Ms. Sara Black, 22 Ridge Rd., Fairmont, WV, 26554; 5-Sincerely yours. **(business letters)**

Page 68, **In the Mail:** **(envelopes)**

Page 69, **Apply Yourself:** **(filling out forms)**

Page 70, **Eating Out:** 2-$.20; 3-$3.20; 4-yes, no; 5-$.40; 6-peanut butter & jelly; 7-lunch 2; 8-friend's, $.25. **(reading a menu)**

Page 71, **The Best Source:** 1-encyclopedia; 2-dictionary; 3-atlas; 4-encyclopedia; 5-dictionary; 6-thesaurus; 7-dictionary; 8-almanac; 9-encyclopedia; 10-atlas; 11-almanac; 12-encyclopedia; 13-atlas; 14-telephone book. **(reference review)**

Page 72, **Take a Trip:** Answers will vary. **(research review)**

Page 73, **Sound Off!:** Answers will vary. **(research & business letter review)**

Page 74, **Believe It or Not:** 1-T; 2-F, started in 1969; 3-T; 4-T; 5-F, over 2 days; 6-F, The Black Death; 7-T; 8-F, took place in 1961; 9-F, took place in NJ; 10-T. **(reference review)**

Super Circus Mystery

The circus was in town!
But something was missing.
Finally the mystery was solved.

Below are the words from the headline of the
morning newspaper. But they are all mixed up.

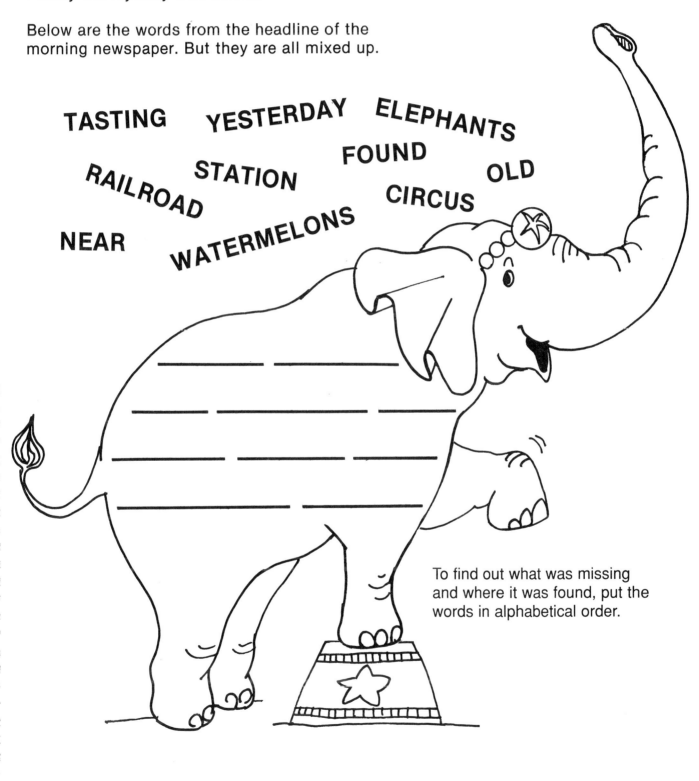

TASTING   YESTERDAY   ELEPHANTS

FOUND

RAILROAD   STATION   OLD

CIRCUS

NEAR   WATERMELONS

To find out what was missing
and where it was found, put the
words in alphabetical order.

Name_____ **Date** _____

1

Priscilla's Peculiar Pet

What kind of pet did
Priscilla want?

The best pet is...

To find out, rewrite the
names of these animals in
alphabetical order.

Circle the same letters
that are circled below.

bea®r

sh®ark

mi®nk

m®uskrat

buff®lo

sku®nk

se®ter

mon®oose

babo®n

1. _____

2. _____

3. _____

4. _____

5. _____

6. _____

7. _____

8. _____

9. _____

When the names are in alphabetical order,
the circled letters will spell the name of
Priscilla's peculiar pet.

¯1¯ ¯2¯ ¯3¯ ¯4¯ ¯5¯   **–**   ¯6¯ ¯7¯ ¯8¯ ¯9¯

Name_____ **Date** _____

Franklin Stein, Monster Maker

Franklin likes to experiment. One day, he decided to make a monster. But something went wrong.

He mixed all kinds of ingredients together, but he didn't make a monster. What did Franklin make?

To find out, put these 12 ingredients in alphabetical order. Circle the same letters that are circled below. Then write the circled letters in the blanks at the bottom.

1. _____

2. _____

3. _____

4. _____

5. _____

6. _____

7. _____

8. _____

9. _____

10. _____

11. _____

12. _____

mayonnaise
mackintosh
bamboo shoots
mammoth lips
mashed beetle feet
mantis wings
badger teeth
mahogany roots
mallard feathers
mare's knees
banana peels
magic beans

Franklin made ___ ___ ___   ___ ___ ___ ___ ___ ___ ___ ___ ___ .
             1 2 3   4 5 6 7 8 9 10 11 12

Name_____ **Date** _____

Look at the Lexicon!

A dictionary gives a great deal of information about words. For each entry word, a dictionary gives the correct spelling, pronunciation, meaning, and part of speech. The *etymology*, or history of the word, may also be shown.

Find the word LEXICON in a dictionary. Then answer the questions below.

1. Which of these pronunciations is correct?

    a. lēk•sĭ•kŏń

    b. lĕk•sī•kən

    c. lĕk•sĭ•kŏń

2. Which of these definitions is accurate?

    a. a bird with six toes

    b. a thesaurus

    c. a dictionary

3. What part of speech is it? _____

4. How is the plural form spelled?

_____

5. What is its etymology?

    a. It comes from a French word.

    b. It dates back to an Old English word.

    c. It can be traced back to a Greek word.

Now use a lexicon to answer these questions:

6. If you had a *papaya,* what would you do with it?

    a) ride it   b) eat it   c) play it

7. If you had a *yew,* what would you do with it?

    a) plant it   b) play with it   c) cook it

8. If you had a *zither,* what would you do with it?

    a) read it   b) drink it   c) play it

There it is!

Dictionary

Name_____ **Date** _____

4

Help the Ground Hog

The guide words on each page of a dictionary tell you the first and last words that are on that page.

Using the guide words below, help the Ground Hog find these words in his dictionary. Decide what page each word will be found on, and write that page number after the word.

Page	Guide Words	Ground Hog's Words	Page
212	**session / shaft**	**slumber**	_____
		squint	_____
219	**shellac / shot**	**shortsighted**	_____
		squirrel	_____
		sunshine	_____
		sleep	_____
221	**slate / smack**	**severe**	_____
		superstition	_____
223	**spread / stable**	**shade**	_____
		sunlight	_____
		springtime	_____
225	**summer / surface**	**shelter**	_____

Now help the Ground Hog find his shadow.
On what page will **shadow** be found?

_____

The Entry Sentry

A dictionary entry is usually printed in dark type. An entry can be a word, a contraction, a country's name, or a person's name. It can be a prefix, a suffix, or an abbreviation. It can even be a single letter.

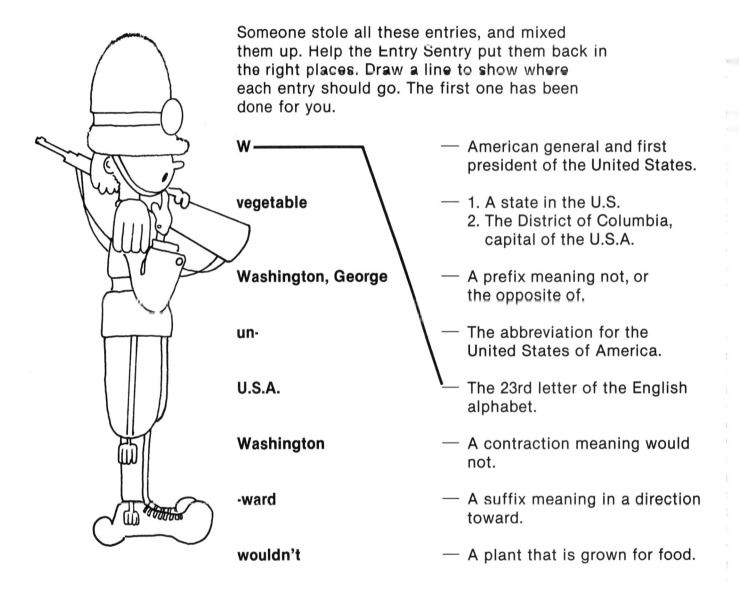

Someone stole all these entries, and mixed them up. Help the Entry Sentry put them back in the right places. Draw a line to show where each entry should go. The first one has been done for you.

W ——— — American general and first president of the United States.

vegetable — 1. A state in the U.S.
2. The District of Columbia, capital of the U.S.A.

Washington, George — A prefix meaning not, or the opposite of.

un- — The abbreviation for the United States of America.

U.S.A. — The 23rd letter of the English alphabet.

Washington — A contraction meaning would not.

-ward — A suffix meaning in a direction toward.

wouldn't — A plant that is grown for food.

Name _____   **Date** _____

Say What?

A dictionary uses pronunciation symbols to show you how each entry is pronounced. The pronunciation symbols are shown in the pronunciation key.

Part of a pronunciation key is shown at the left. Use it to match each word with its correct pronunciation.

symbol	sound
ā	face
ă	map
b	**bib**
ch	**church**
d	**did**
ē	**bee, sea**
ĕ	bed, thread
f	**fifty, laugh, ph**ase
ī	**ice, pie,** by
ĭ	it
j	**jet, edge**
k	**kick**
l	let, hand**le**
m	**mom**
n	**n**i**n**e
ō	**joke, toe,** alth**ough**
ô	paw, caught
p	**pop**
r	**rare**
s	**set, face**
t	**tip, pit**
ŭ	**up,** en**ough**
z	**zip,** xylophone, laces

ape

bowl

beach

clap

cone

fawn

bread

gym

knit

night

rough

bōl

klăp

āp

bēch

fôn

jĭm

kōn

brĕd

nīt

rŭf

nĭt

Syl•la•ble Pi•rate Hunt

Say each word.
Ask yourself how many
syllables it has.
Then look up each word
in a dictionary.
Draw a line between the
syllables.
The one below has already
been done for you.

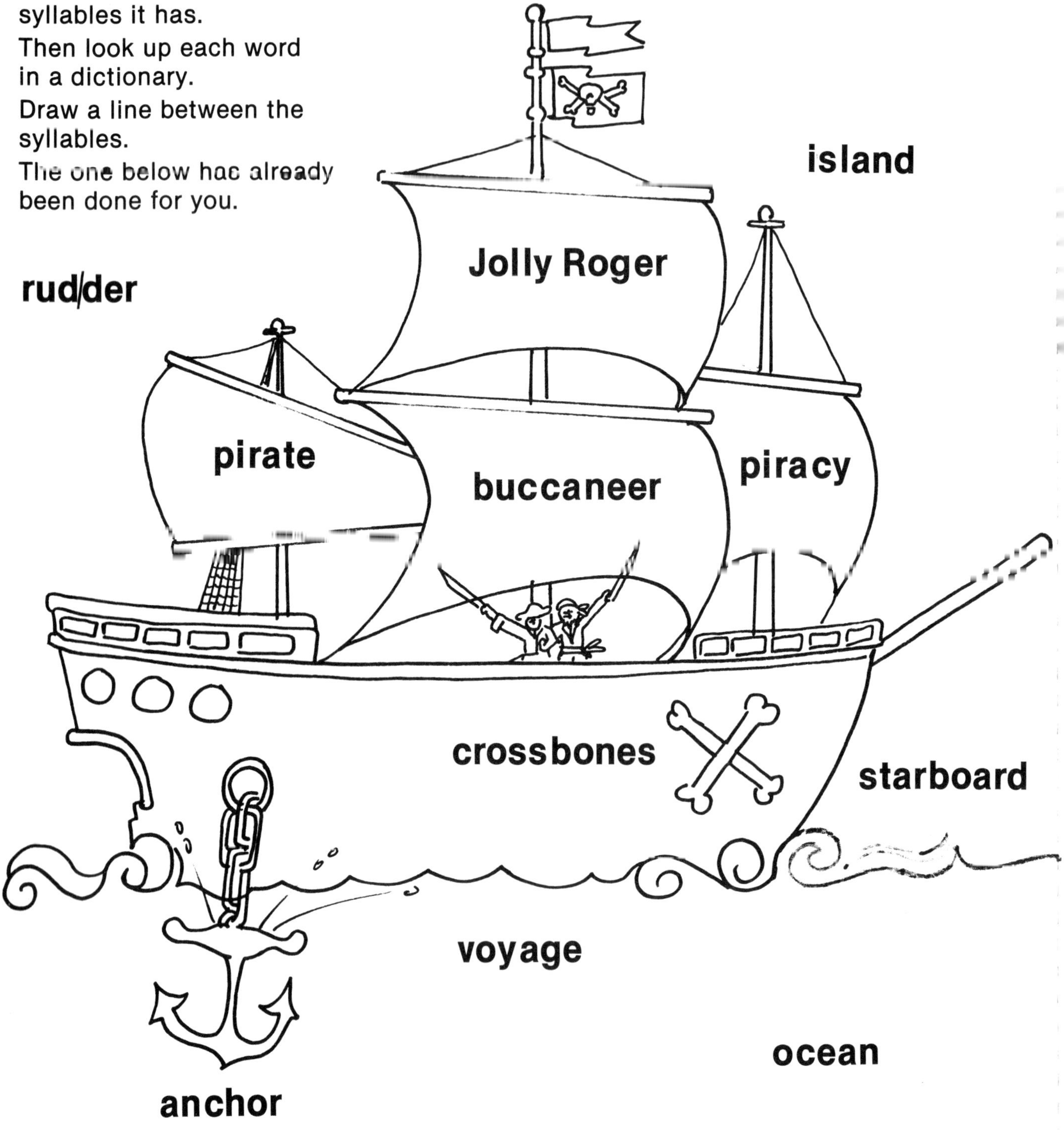

island

Jolly Roger

rud/der

pirate

buccaneer

piracy

crossbones

starboard

voyage

ocean

anchor

Name_____

Date_____

Ac•ro•bat Ac•cents

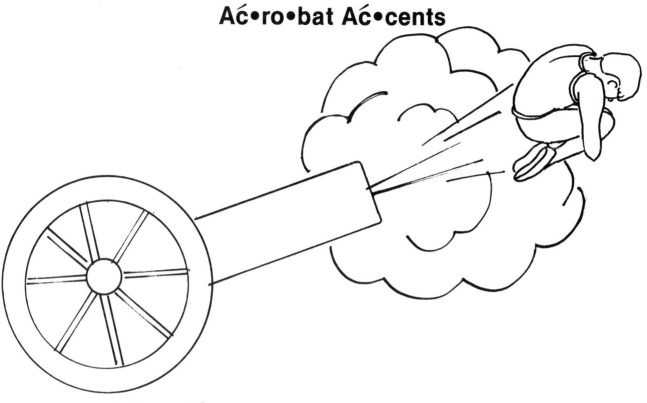

at•trac•tions   pa•rade

au•di•ence   per•form•ance

cir•cus   spec•tac•u•lar

jug•gler   stu•pen•dous

me•nag•er•ie   tra•peze

Help the ringmaster pronounce the words correctly.
Say each word out loud. Which syllable did you say loudest?
Put an accent mark over the syllable, like this:

el•e•phant

When you have finished, look up each word in a dictionary.
Did you put the accent on the right syllable?

Name_____ **Date** _____

9

The Ghostly Schwa

This symbol ə is called the schwa. The schwa sound is the vowel
sound heard in many syllables that are not stressed, like the first
syllable of *around* or the last syllable of *sofa*.
Any vowel can make the schwa sound.

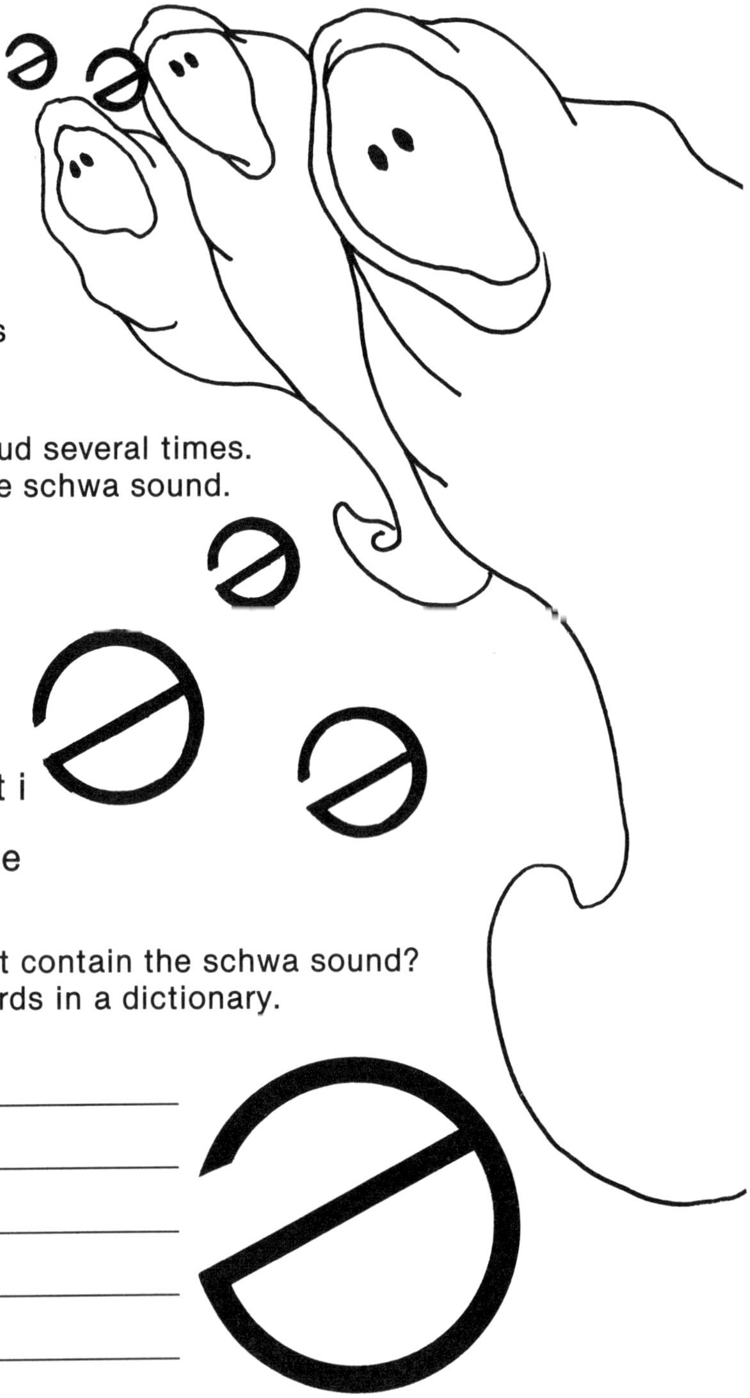

Examples:

a as in ahead	ə•hed
e as in item	i•təm
i as in giraffe	jə•raf
o as in pilot	pi•lət
u as in focus	fo•kəs

Say each of the following words out loud several times.
Circle the letter or letters that make the schwa sound.

a f r a i d	c a b o o s e
c e r a m i c s	c o c o o n
c o l l a p s e	m i l i t i a
s h e l l a c	s p a g h e t t i
s u p p o s e	s u s p e n s e

Can you think of some other words that contain the schwa sound?
Write five of them here. Check your words in a dictionary.

_____

_____

_____

_____

_____

Name_____ **Date** _____

10

Loony Laughs

**A dictionary entry shows what part of speech a word is.
Many dictionaries use abbreviations for the parts of speech.**

Draw a line to match each part of speech with its abbreviation.

noun	adj.
verb	v.
adjective	n.
adverb	pron.
pronoun	adv.
preposition	conj.
conjunction	interj.
interjection	prep.

Now use a dictionary to find out what part of speech
each of these words is:

1. alas _____
2. into _____
3. loon _____
4. swiftly _____
5. generalize _____
6. we _____
7. marvelous _____
8. and _____
9. finicky _____
10. hurdy-gurdy _____
11. reflect _____
12. hurrah _____

Name_____ Date _____

Help Inez Pick

Inez wants to know which dictionary entry gives
the meaning for the underlined word in each sentence.
Can you help her?

Read each sentence. Decide what part of speech the
underlined word is. (Is it a noun, a verb, an adjective,
or an adverb?)

Then help Inez pick the right dictionary definition by
circling it. The first one has already been done for you.

1. Mrs. Jackson had to <u>back</u> the car out of the
driveway before she could go to the store.

back noun—The part of the body on the
opposite side from the chest.
back verb—To move in a reverse direction.

2. After a <u>brief</u> delay, everyone lined up at the
starting line.

brief adj.—Short
brief verb—To give instructions or advice.

3. The <u>chief</u> reason we lost the game was that
we did not try hard enough.

chief noun—A leader or boss.
chief adj.—Most important.

4. The water at the lake was much too <u>cold</u>
to swim in.

cold adj.—Having a low temperature.
cold noun—A sickness with sneezing,
coughing, fever, and chills.

5. A good detective must <u>comb</u> through all
the evidence and look for more clues.

comb noun—A thin object with teeth, used to
smooth and arrange the hair.
comb verb—To search thoroughly.

6. Sylvia's new jacket was filled with
<u>down</u>.

down adv.—Toward the ground.
down noun—Soft fluffy feathers.

7. After the boat tipped over, Beth and Barry
tried to <u>right</u> it again.

right adj.—Correct or true.
right verb—To turn right-side-up.

8. The mountain climbers wanted to <u>scale</u> the
last peak before darkness fell.

scale noun—Something used for weighing.
scale verb—To climb up or over something.

Name_____ **Date** _____

See You at Sea

Homophones are two or more words that have the same pronunciation, but different spellings and meanings.

Do you know which homophone belongs in each of the sentences in the story below?

Look up each pair of homophones in a dictionary. Circle the one that should be used in each sentence. Then turn the paper over and use the homophones in your own sentences.

The peculiar pirates raised the (sail, sale) on their boat and lifted the anchor. The wind quickly (blew, blue) the boat out to sea. The sky was clear, except for a few clouds (hi, high) overhead. Since there was plenty to do, no one was (board, bored).

Later, one of the pirates told a (tale, tail) about a treasure that was guarded by a skeleton. The (hole, whole) crew listened with interest to the story. "Some day," said the pirate, "that buried treasure will be (hours, ours)!"

Finally the (sun, son) began to set, and the sky slowly grew dark. Soon, (knight, night) had fallen, and everyone went to sleep. They all knew that this was going to be a (great, grate) adventure.

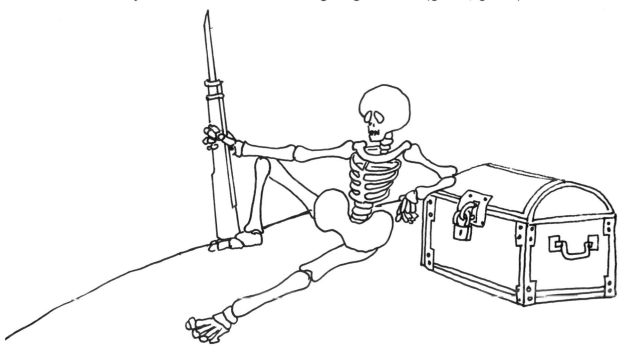

Name_____ Date _____

Synonym Sleuth

Synonyms are words that have similar meanings.

Use a dictionary to look up the meanings of the following words. Then write a synonym next to each word. Choose from the list at the bottom.

As you write each synonym, circle the same letter that was circled before. Then write the circled letters in order to solve the secret message below.

davenport　　1.＿＿＿＿＿＿＿＿＿

pharmacist　　2.＿＿＿＿＿＿＿＿＿

carousel　　3.＿＿＿＿＿＿＿＿＿

instruct　　4.＿＿＿＿＿＿＿＿＿

kin　　5.＿＿＿＿＿＿＿＿＿

clarity　　6.＿＿＿＿＿＿＿＿＿

specter　　7.＿＿＿＿＿＿＿＿＿

captive　　8.＿＿＿＿＿＿＿＿＿

hamlet　　9.＿＿＿＿＿＿＿＿＿

novice　　10.＿＿＿＿＿＿＿＿＿

**Secret Message:
A sleuth is**

‾
1

‾　‾　‾　‾　‾　‾　‾　‾　‾
2　3　4　5　6　7　8　9　10

beginn(e)r　　pr(i)soner
(c)learness　　relativ(e)
(d)ruggist　　sof(a)
ghos(t)　　(t)each
m(e)rry-go-round　　(v)illage

Hi!

B

Say It Again with Synonyms

Salutations!

W

Bill and William are cousins. They always use different words to say the same thing. For example, Bill says, "I washed my face," but William says, "I bathed my visage."

What Bill says is in the left-hand column. Use a thesaurus, a dictionary of synonyms, to decide what William might have said instead. Write the letter on the line.

Bill	**William**
1. burn the candle _____	a) ancient as the hummocks
2. fast as the wind _____	b) behold an apparition
3. fat as an elephant _____	c) comely as a portrait
4. old as the hills _____	d) corpulent as a pachyderm
5. pretty as a picture _____	e) incinerate the taper
6. see a ghost _____	f) rapid as a zephyr

When you have finished, you may want to do these, just for fun!

7. ring the bells _____	g) peruse a tome
8. read a book _____	h) petrous as a monolith
9. sharp as a tack _____	i) keen as a brad
10. snake in the grass _____	j) strike the carillon
11. hard as a rock_____	k) viper in the pasturage
12. rich as a king _____	l) affluent as a monarch

Name_____ Date _____

Aunt O. Nym Needs Help

Antonyms are words with opposite meanings.
Slow and *fast* are antonyms. So are *smooth* and *rough*. And so are *gigantic* and *tiny*.

Poor Aunt O. Nym! She needs an antonym for each of these words. Can you help her?

Draw a line to match each word in Aunt O. Nym's list with an antonym from the list at the right. If you are not sure what any word means, look it up in a dictionary.

Aunt O. Nym's List	**Antonyms**
entrance	guilty
innocent	youthful
aged	exit
wrong	unsure
certain	correct
indistinct	easy
delay	hurry
difficult	clear
serious	skinny
obese	funny

Name_____ Date _____

Short & Sweet

**An abbreviation is the shortened form that represents a word or group of words.
For example, *U.S.A.* is the abbreviation for *United States of America*.**

Find each of the following abbreviations in a dictionary. Write down the word or group of words each abbreviation represents.

cm _____

C.O.D. _____

D.D.S. _____

doz. _____

E.S.T. _____

Feb. _____

H.M.S. _____

lb _____

Mr. _____

neg. _____

N.Y.C. _____

oz _____

plu. _____

R.N. _____

Sat. _____

syn. _____

U.N. _____

KILLER KELLER, D.D.S.
The
Sweet Tooth
Puller

HONEY
8oz

Name _____ **Date** _____

Pelican Plurals

**If a plural is not formed by adding *S* or *ES* to the
singular form, the dictionary will usually show
you how to spell the plural form.**

Peggy the Pelican wants to know the plurals of
these words. Can you help her? Look up each
word in your dictionary. Write the plural on the line.
Some words have more than one plural.

1. antenna _____

2. axis _____

3. buffalo _____

4. cherry _____

5. child _____

6. deer _____

7. elf _____

8. fish _____

9. foot _____

10. goose _____

11. knife _____

12. larva _____

13. man-of-war _____

14. moose _____

15. mouse _____

16. ox _____

17. wife _____

18. wolf _____

Isabelle's Idioms

An idiom is a phrase or group of words with a special meaning. Its meaning is different from the meaning of the individual words. An idiom is usually listed in a dictionary under the most important word in the phrase.

Isabelle wants to know what these idioms mean. Can you help her? See how many of these idioms you can find in a standard dictionary. Write the meanings on the lines below. Circle the word you found each idiom listed under.

1. let the cat
   out of the bag _____

2. see eye to eye _____

3. from the horse's mouth _____

4. in hot water _____

5. turn over a new leaf _____

6. wet behind the ears _____

7. wet your whistle _____

8. turn the tables _____

9. at the drop of a hat _____

10. change your tune _____

Now choose one of the idioms. Draw a funny picture on the back of this sheet to illustrate it!

Name_____ Date _____

Dizzy Definitions

When a word has more than one meaning, a dictionary will list each meaning, or definition, after the entry.

Three definitions are listed for each word below. Two are correct, but the third is "dizzy"—it is not a real definition for the word.

Use a dictionary to find out which two definitions are real. Then circle the number for the definition that is "dizzy."

1. **cobbler**
   1. a person who mends shoes
   2. a fruit pie baked in a deep dish
   3. a machine that takes corn off the cob

2. **crane**
   1. a blanket made of cotton and nylon
   2. a machine with a long arm for lifting things
   3. a bird with a long neck and long legs

3. **girth**
   1. a measurement around something
   2. a sign on the front of a store
   3. a strap that keeps a saddle on a horse

4. **gondola**
   1. a walking stick used by hikers in the Swiss Alps
   2. a low, open freight car used on a railroad
   3. a long, narrow boat used on the canals in Venice

5. **nutcracker**
   1. a tool for cracking open the shells of nuts
   2. a cracker or cookie that contains nuts
   3. a bird that feeds on nuts

6. **pommel**
   1. the rounded knob on the handle of a sword
   2. the horn on the saddle of a horse
   3. the eye in the end of a sewing needle

7. **ruffle**
   1. to salute a uniformed officer
   2. to disturb or annoy someone
   3. to wrinkle something, or make it uneven

8. **stand**
   1. a small booth or other place where goods are offered for sale
   2. a tall, narrow, natural monument on the floor of a cave or a cavern
   3. a group of growing trees or plants

Name_____ Date _____

Flora & Fauna

Flora likes *plants* of all kinds. She wrote down the names of ten different plants.

Fauna prefers *animals* of all kinds. He wrote down the names of ten different animals.

But someone mixed all the names together. Now Flora and Fauna need some help to separate them. Look up each name in a dictionary. Write the plants on Flora's list, and the animals on Fauna's list.

basenji
chamois
indigo
kite
leek
lichen
loon
okra
phlox
phoebe
rhea
rook
sedge
tapir
thyme
vanilla
whelk
woodbine
yucca
zebu

Name_____ **Date**_____

What's in a Name?

**Many dictionaries include the names of famous or important people. They are
usually listed alphabetically, last name first, along with the other entries.**

Use a dictionary to find out about each person whose name is listed below.
Then write the letter of the correct description after each person's name.

Louisa May Alcott _____

Benedict Arnold _____

Richard Evelyn Byrd _____

Emily Elizabeth Dickinson _____

Sigmund Freud _____

Alexander Hamilton _____

Helen Adams Keller _____

Frances Perkins _____

Beatrix Potter _____

Emma Lazarus _____

Claude Monet _____

Eli Whitney _____

a) American poet, 1830–1886

b) American admiral and polar explorer, 1888–1957

c) American author, 1832–1888

d) Austrian neurologist and founder of psychoanalysis, 1856–1939

e) American Revolutionary War general and traitor, 1741–1801

f) American statesman and first U.S. Secretary of the Treasury, 1755–1804

g) American poet and philanthropist, 1849–1887

h) American social worker and first woman cabinet member as Secretary of Labor, 1882–1965

i) English author, illustrator, and creator of Peter Rabbit, 1866–1943

j) Blind and deaf American author and speaker, 1880–1968

k) American inventor of the cotton gin, 1765–1825

l) French painter, 1840–1926

Name_____ Date _____

At the Zoo

Pretend you are going to spend a day at the zoo. To find your way around you'll need to be able to read a map. Use the map key and the map to help you answer these questions.

1. What does this symbol ⛄ stand for? _____

2. Is the first aid station closer to the Children's Zoo or to the hippos? _____

3. You are at the seal exhibit. Put an X on the restroom closest to you.

Use the compass rose and the map to help you fill in the directions below.
Write N, S, E, W, NE, SE, NW, or SW.

4. To get from the monkeys to the gorillas you have to walk _____.

5. The Children's Zoo is _____ of the seals.

6. The hippos are _____ of the bears.

7. If you are at the Children's Zoo and you want to see the bears, which way will you walk? _____

8. The bears are in what direction from the seals? _____

9. To get from the hippos to the first aid station, which way will you walk? _____

10. To go from the bears to the parking lot, you must go _____.

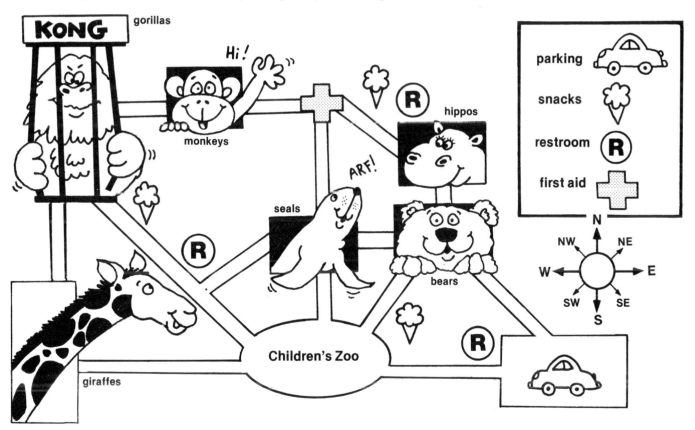

Name_____ Date _____

Tangleberry's Treasure

Tangleberry hid a terrific treasure and marked the location on this map. To find out what the treasure was, complete the statements and answer the questions below. Choose from the following words:

Appleton   marsh
Bongo Bay   railroad
east   river
Gap   south
highway   Ugly's

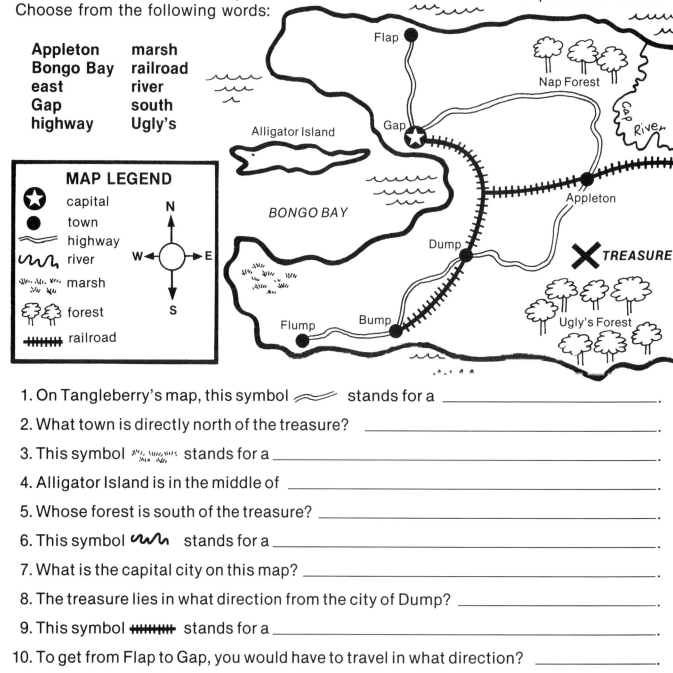

1. On Tangleberry's map, this symbol ⌇ stands for a _____.

2. What town is directly north of the treasure? _____.

3. This symbol ⁘⁘⁘ stands for a _____.

4. Alligator Island is in the middle of _____.

5. Whose forest is south of the treasure? _____.

6. This symbol ∿ stands for a _____.

7. What is the capital city on this map? _____.

8. The treasure lies in what direction from the city of Dump? _____.

9. This symbol ┼┼┼┼┼ stands for a _____.

10. To get from Flap to Gap, you would have to travel in what direction? _____.

Now write the first letter of each answer in the correct space below, and you will spell the name of Tangleberry's treasure.

___   ___   ___   ___   ___   ___   ___   ___   ___   ___
1   2   3   4   5   6   7   8   9   10

Name_____   Date_____

Map Sense

The map on this page shows the state of Washington. Use it to help you decide whether or not the sentences below are correct. If a sentence is correct, circle the number of the sentence. If a sentence is incorrect, cross out the underlined word and write the correct word on the line provided.

1. Idaho and <u>Canada</u> are two states that border Washington. _____

2. The <u>Atlantic</u> Ocean is west of Washington. _____

3. <u>Seattle</u> is the country north of Washington. _____

4. The southernmost city shown on the map is <u>Vancouver</u>. _____

5. The longest river in Washington is the <u>Snake</u> River. _____

6. The capital of Washington is <u>Tacoma</u>. _____

7. Seattle is <u>northwest</u> of Olympia. _____

8. The Okanogan River runs <u>north</u> and <u>south</u>. _____

9. The <u>Rocky</u> Mountains separate eastern and western Washington. _____

10. The mountains in the northwest part of Washington are the <u>Olympic</u> Mountains. _____

11. Mt. Ranier is the highest mountain in the state. It is southeast of Seattle and Tacoma. It is part of the <u>Cascade</u> Mountains. _____

12. Vancouver Island is a <u>Canadian</u> island. _____

13. The Rocky Mountains are in the <u>northeast</u> part of Washington. _____

14. The <u>Yakima</u> River provides part of Washington's border with Oregon. _____

Make an outline map of your state. Use the map symbols below and show your state's borders, capital, large cities, rivers, and mountains.

Name_____ Date _____

Candytown Little League

There are five teams in the Candytown Little League. In all, they will play a total of 20 games. The chart below shows when each game is scheduled to be played. It also shows who plays against whom, which team is the home team, and which team is the visiting team.

The home teams are listed on the left side of the chart.

The visiting teams are listed along the top of the chart.

The dates of the games are shown in the boxes.

Candytown Little League Baseball Schedule

HOME TEAM	Gumdrops	Peppermints	Chocolates	Jellybeans	Licorice Sticks
Gumdrops		JULY 2	JUNE 21	JUNE 23	JULY 7
Peppermints	JUNE 25		JULY 6	JUNE 27	JUNE 30
Chocolates	JUNE 29	JULY 8		JULY 1	JUNE 24
Jellybeans	JULY 5	JULY 10	JULY 3		JUNE 28
Licorice Sticks	JULY 9	JUNE 22	JUNE 26	JULY 4	

(VISITING TEAM listed along the top)

Use the chart to find the answers to the following questions.

1. The chart shows that the Gumdrops will be the home team on July 2, June 21, June 23, and July 7. Who will be the **visiting team** in the July 7 game? _____

2. The Peppermints will be the visiting team in a game on July 10. Who will be the **home team** on that date? _____

3. When will the Chocolates be the home team, playing against the Gumdrops? _____

4. On what two dates will the Licorice Sticks and the Peppermints play against each other? _____

5. What two teams will play on the Fourth of July?
_____ and _____

Name_____   **Date** _____

26

Picture That!

The George Washington School just had its annual book fair. The graphs on this page give some information about the books sold at the fair. Use each graph to answer the questions next to it.

A picture graph uses pictures to show information. This picture graph shows how many books were bought by students in the fifth grade.

BOOKS BOUGHT

Class	Books Bought
5A	⊞ ⊞ ⊞ ⊞ ⊞ ⊞ ⊞ ⊞
5B	⊞ ⊞ ⊞ ⊞ ⊞
5C	⊞ ⊞ ⊞ ⊞ ⊞ ⊞

⊞ = four books

1. Which class bought the most books?
   _____

2. Which class bought the least books?
   _____

3. How many books were bought by the students in class 5C? _____

4. How many books were bought by the students in class 5B? _____

5. What is the total number of books bought by the fifth grade? _____

A line graph uses lines to show information. This line graph shows the number of books sold at the book fair each day.

6. On which day were the most books sold? _____

7. On which day were the least books sold? _____

8. On which two days were the same number of books sold? _____

9. Were more books sold on Wednesday or Monday? _____

10. How many books were sold on Tuesday? _____

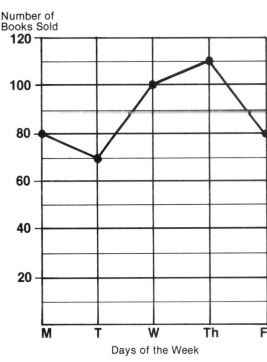

Number of
Books Sold

Days of the Week

Name_____ Date _____

At a Glance

DISTANCES ANIMALS CAN JUMP

Hi!

Kangaroo
Horse
Human
Jack rabbit
Hare
Frog
Grasshopper

| 4 (1.2) | 8 (2.4) | 12 (3.6) | 16 (4.8) | 20 (6.1) | 24 (7.3) | 28 (8.5) | 32 (9.7) | 36 (11) | 40 (12.1) | 44 (13.3) |

Number of Feet
(Meters in parentheses)

A bar graph uses bars to show information. The length of the bar shows the amount of what is being measured. The bar graph above shows how far certain animals can jump. Use it to answer these questions.

1. Which animal can jump the farthest? _____

2. Which animal jumps the shortest distance? _____

3. Which animal can jump father—a hare or a jack rabbit? _____

4. How far can a kangaroo jump? _____

5. About how far can a frog jump? _____

6. Which animals can jump farther than a human?_____

Make a bar graph to show which bands your friends like best. Choose four popular bands. Ask each of ten friends who his or her favorite band is. Then fill in the bars to show the number of people who liked each band best.

NAMES
OF BANDS

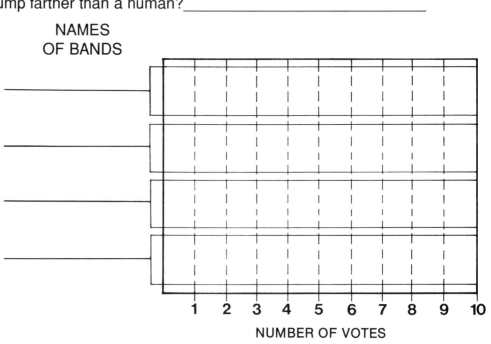

| 1 | 2 | 3 | 4 | 5 | 6 | 7 | 8 | 9 | 10 |

NUMBER OF VOTES

Name_____ **Date** _____

Ghosts, Ghouls, & Goblins

Gail and Gary made this line graph to show how many ghosts, ghouls, and goblins lived in the old haunted house since 1900.

Use the graph to find the answers to the following questions.

1. How many ghosts were there in 1920? _____

2. In what year were there equal numbers of ghosts and goblins? _____

3. In 1950, which group had the largest population? _____

4. From 1910 to 1920, which group showed a decrease? _____

5. From 1950 to 1960, which group showed the largest increase? _____

6. In 1970, which group had the lowest population? _____

7. In 1940, how many ghosts, ghouls, and goblins were there all together? _____

8. Suppose you counted 4 ghosts, 7 ghouls, and 10 goblins in 2000. Can you add those statistics to the graph? Do it.

Name_____ **Date** _____

Silly Star Olympics

Each year, the Silly Stars try to beat each other in silly events at the Silly Star Olympics. These bar graphs show the results of two events from this year's Olympics. Answer the questions next to each graph.

HAND WALK CONTEST

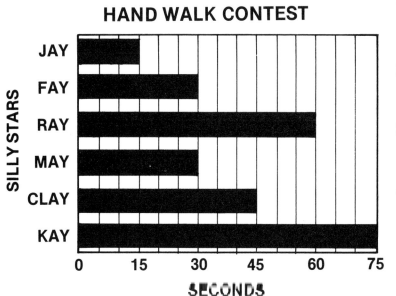

SILLY STARS

JAY
FAY
RAY
MAY
CLAY
KAY

0   15   30   45   60   75

SECONDS

1. Who did the hand walk for the longest time? _____

2. Who did the hand walk for 15 seconds? _____

3. For how many seconds did Clay do his hand walk? _____

4. Who came in second, and how many seconds was that person's hand walk? _____
_____

5. In the Slippery Pole Climb, how high did the winner climb? _____

6. What two Silly Stars climbed to the same height? _____ and _____

7. How much higher did Zoe climb than Bo?
_____

8. Who came in last in the Slippery Pole Climb?
_____

SLIPPERY POLE CLIMB

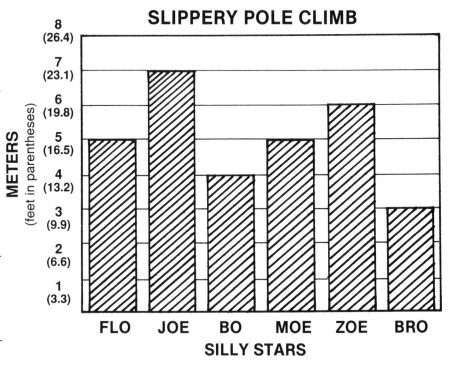

METERS
(feet in parentheses)

8 (26.4)
7 (23.1)
6 (19.8)
5 (16.5)
4 (13.2)
3 (9.9)
2 (6.6)
1 (3.3)

FLO   JOE   BO   MOE   ZOE   BRO

SILLY STARS

Name_____   Date_____

Going Around in Circles

A circle graph is divided into wedges, or slices, to show the different parts of the whole.

Vanessa made the circle graph at the right to show how she spends an average day.

1. What does Vanessa spend the most time doing? _____

2. The smallest amount of Vanessa's time is spent in what way? _____

3. Which takes more of Vanessa's time: hobbies or homework? _____

HOW EACH DAY IS SPENT

**WHERE EACH DOLLAR WENT
Last Year**

Victor made two circle graphs to compare the way he spent each dollar of his allowance last year with this year.

4. What took the smallest portion of Victor's allowance last year? _____

5. What took the smallest portion of his allowance this year? _____

6. Did Victor spend a larger or a smaller portion of his allowance on the movies this year compared to last year? _____

7. How much of each dollar did Victor put into savings this year? _____

8. Did he save more or less of each dollar last year, compared to this year? _____

This Year

Name_____   Date _____

Time for a Time Line

A time line arranges events in the order in which they occurred.

Read the following paragraph, and study the time line. Then answer the questions below.

The United States has expanded its boundaries in many ways. In the Treaty of Paris, which ended the Revolutionary War in 1783, the U.S. gained land that extended its western boundary to the Mississippi River. This was called the Addition of 1783. Territory gained through other treaties included the Red River Cession of 1818, the Florida Cession of 1819, the Oregon Country Cession of 1846, and the Mexican Cession of 1848. Land purchased from other countries included the Louisiana Purchase of 1803, the Gadsden Purchase of 1853, and the Alaska Purchase of 1867. Texas was annexed, or added, in 1845, and Hawaii was annexed in 1898.

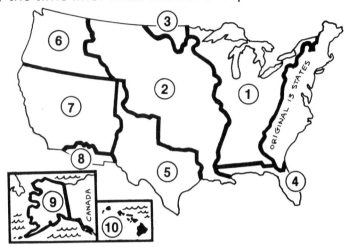

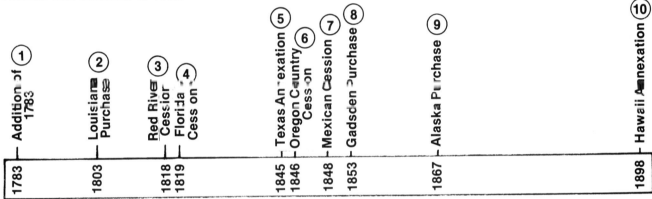

1. Which came first, the Texas Annexation, or the Florida Cession? _____

2. The Gadsden Purchase occurred how many years after the Mexican Cession? _____

3. When Alaska was purchased, did the U.S. already include the Oregon Country? _____

4. Was any territory added to the U.S. between the Addition of 1783 and the Louisiana

   Purchase? _____

5. The last expansion of U.S. boundaries occurred in what year? _____

6. What was the first territorial expansion to take place after the Louisiana Purchase?

   _____

Name _____ **Date** _____

It's All in the Almanac

Up-to-date information, tables, and statistics on a wide range of subjects can be found in an almanac. To find the facts you need, just look up the subject in the index at the back of the almanac.

What subject could you look under to find the answer to each of these questions? Write the subjects in column A. If you have an almanac, find the answers and write them in Column B.

	Column A	**Column B**

1. What major-league baseball player holds the record for the most home runs in a season? _____ _____

2. Who was the Women's Singles Tennis Champion at Wimbledon last year? _____ _____

3. When did the first U.S. manned space flight take place? _____ _____

4. What is the height of the tallest mountain in the world? _____ _____

5. Which team in the National Football League won the most recent Super Bowl game? _____ _____

6. If you were on the smallest continent in the world, where would you be? _____ _____

Name_____ **Date** _____

Bird Watching

The list below may look like something a bird watcher would use. But each name on the list is also the name of at least one town, county, mountain or peak located in the United States or Canada.

Look up each name in an atlas (a book of maps) and find out where it is. Then identify it, and give its location.

1. CARDINAL _____

2. CRANE _____

3. CROW _____

4. DUCK _____

5. EAGLE _____

_____

6. JAY _____

_____

7. MARTIN _____

_____

_____

8. OSPREY _____

9. PELICAN _____

10. PIGEON _____

11. RAVEN _____

12. SWIFT _____

13. TURKEY _____

Hill Street Clues

The kids on Hill Street have a few tricky questions.
They know that all the answers are in the encyclopedia.
But what subjects should they look under to find them?

One key word in each question is the clue that leads to the answer. Which word should
they look up? Circle the clues for the Hill Street kids.

1. Does a giraffe have two toes or three toes?

2. What kind of food does an octopus eat?

3. What is the best time of year to pick apples ?

4. Are tears really made of salt water?

5. What kinds of animals are found only in
   Australia ?

6. If a lizard loses its tail, can it grow a
   new one?

7. How many keys are there on a piano ?

8. Are all airships filled with the same kind
   of gas?

9. Is there any kind of bird that cannot fly?

10. What is the temperature on the surface of the sun ?

Know It All
ENCYCLOPEDIA
L

Name_____ Date _____

That's News to Me!

Newspapers contain information that is more recent than that found in encyclopedias, almanacs, and other reference books.

Circle the information you would probably find only in a newspaper.

1. The names of the football teams that played in the first Super Bowl.

2. The score of yesterday's tennis match.

3. The names of the candidates who are running for the presidency.

4. The number of years a state senator is normally elected to serve.

5. Tho forocast for tomorrow's weather.

6. The results of a recent public opinion survey.

7. The dates the Pony Express started and stopped operating.

8. The names of the movies appearing in local theaters this weekend.

9. The names of the 10 largest lakes in the world.

10. The price of a head of lettuce in the supermarket

11. The score of the last baseball game played in the 1975 World Series.

12. Up-to-date stock market quotations.

Name_____ **Date** _____

Be an Editor

Imagine that you are the editor of a newspaper. On your desk are items for the next edition. In which section will you place each one— *Book Review, Classified, Editorial, Entertainment, Financial, News, Sports,* or *Weather*?

Study the items below. Then write the name of the section on the line.

1. Stock prices advanced moderately yesterday. _____

2. The Mayor presented the governor with the keys to the city today. _____

3. *The Tale of Two Tattlers* by Penn Name is the most unusual mystery I've read this year. _____

4. Last night, in the closest game of the season, the Vikings beat the Captains by a score of 101 to 100. _____

5. Motocross Bicycle. Like new $200. _____

6. Continued rain today through Friday. _____

7. An unusual group of handmade puppets can now be seen at the Art Museum. _____

8. Mrs. Smith writes a letter to the editor complaining about dogs in the city park. _____

Read through your local newspaper. Find, clip, and label an item to represent each feature category above.

Name_____ **Date** _____

Where Should We Shop?

☘ Manny's Market ☘

napkins _____	$1.25/50
paper cups_____	2.29/100 5 oz cups
spaghetti _____	2 8-oz boxes 1.99
lemonade_____	6 oz frozen 65¢
strawberries _____	1.69 pint
iceberg lettuce _____	79¢ head
apples _____	59¢ lb
potatoes_____	5 lb bag/1.99
eggs_____	1.09 doz.
orange juice _____	2.69 half gal.
milk _____	79¢ quart
margarine_____	1.59 lb
ice cream _____	1.89 qt.
ground beef _____	2.69 lb

☆ QUICK STOP ☆

napkins _____	$1.45/50
paper cups_____	2.39/100 5 oz cups
spaghetti _____	2 8-oz boxes 1.55
lemonade_____	6 oz frozen 65¢
strawberries _____	1.79 pint
iceberg lettuce _____	69¢ head
apples _____	49¢ lb
potatoes_____	10 lb bag/2.89
eggs_____	99¢ doz.
orange juice _____	2.49 half gal.
milk _____	quarts 2/1.07
margarine_____	1.79 lb
ice cream _____	2.79 qt.
ground beef _____	2.79 lb

The students in Mr. Wall's class have to shop for their class party. Each student can only shop in one store. Use the food ads to help them decide in which stores they will get the best buys. Write the store names on the lines provided.

I'm going to bake cookies.
I need margarine and eggs.

I'm going to bring napkins.
I need at least 75.

I'm going to bring paper
cups.

I'm going to make fruit punch. I need orange
juice, lemonade, and strawberries.

_____   _____

Now do some comparison shopping for yourself. At which store would you get a better buy on each of these items?

iceberg lettuce _____

spaghetti _____

2 quarts milk _____

ground beef _____

Mabel's Tables

The Table of Contents is at the front of a book and lists the subject matter covered inside. It may include chapter titles, broad general topics, and subtopics. The contents are listed in the same order in which they appear in the book.

Study this Table of Contents. Then answer the questions below.

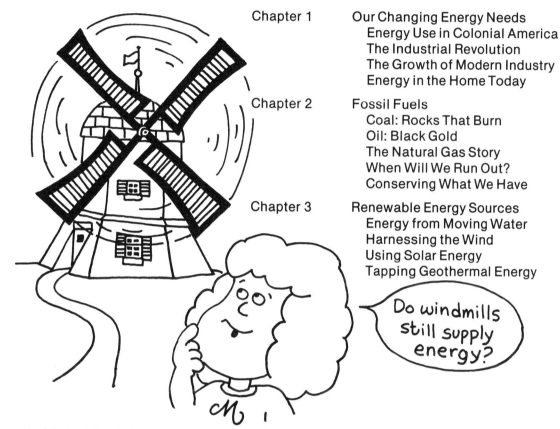

Do windmills still supply energy?

1. Mabel is doing a report on solar energy. On what pages will she find useful information? _____

2. If she wanted to find out about where natural gas is found, what page would she turn to? _____

3. In what chapter would she find information about all kinds of fossil fuels? _____

4. Mabel wants to know if windmills are still used to supply energy. What page should she turn to? _____

5. Next, she must do a report on the amount of energy an athlete would use in performing activities such as swimming, jogging, and playing football. Will this book help her? _____

6. On what pages will she find information for a report on how energy was affected by the Industrial Revolution? _____

The Index Points the Way

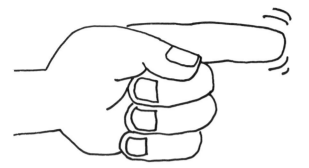

Many reference sources have an index at the back. An index is an alphabetical list of each name, place, and subject that is covered in the book. Following each entry in the index is a list of page numbers on which that name, place, or subject appears.

Here is part of an index. Use it to answer the questions. ↓

Magnetism, 218–55
Minerals, 254, 256, 261
Molds, 135–37, 148
   used as medicines, 159, 160
Moon, 102–32
   craters on, 123, 125–27, 129
   location of, 103, 122
   movement of, 111, 114–19
   phases of, 113, 114, 116, 118
   reflected light of, 104–07, 112–19
     262, 286
   seas of, 121, 123, 124
   seen from earth, 102, 107, 114–19,
     123
   size of, 102, 103
Mountains, 255–57

1. If you were doing a report on the moon, would you find much information in this book?

_____

2. Will this book contain any information about Mars?

_____

3. On what pages will you find information about how doctors use molds to fight disease?

_____

4. If you were doing a report on different kinds of minerals and where they are found, what pages would you read?

_____

5. Will this book help you to prepare a report on magnets and magnetism? _____

6. Suppose you wanted to know how large the moon is. On what pages would you look?

_____

7. You need some information about lunar craters. Where will you find the information?

   List the pages. _____

Name _____ **Date** _____

40

Make a Note of It!

Taking notes is an important study skill. When you take notes, write down only the most important facts. Use your own words. Use abbreviations, if you wish. Try to keep your notes brief.

Pretend you are listening to a talk that is being given by Professor Reginald Reptilian. You want to use some of this information for a report of your own, so you decide to take notes.

Use the space at the bottom of the page to jot down the most important facts. Keep your notes simple.

"Today, I will talk about reptiles. Reptiles are animals such as alligators, lizards, snakes, and turtles.

All reptiles are cold-blooded. This means their temperature changes with the temperature of their surroundings.

Every reptile also has a backbone. Because of this, reptiles are vertebrate animals. Other vertebrates include the fish, the amphibians, the birds, and the mammals.

Reptiles live on land and breathe through lungs. When they swim under the water, they must come to the surface to breathe.

Some people think snakes, lizards, and other reptiles are slimy, but this is not true at all. Their skin is dry and covered with scales."

Name_____ Date _____

Dora's Dogs

Dora had to stand up in front of the whole class and give an oral report. She was afraid she would get mixed up and forget what she wanted to say, so she made an outline that had three main topics. Each main topic had two subtopics. She had the outline in front of her when she gave her report.

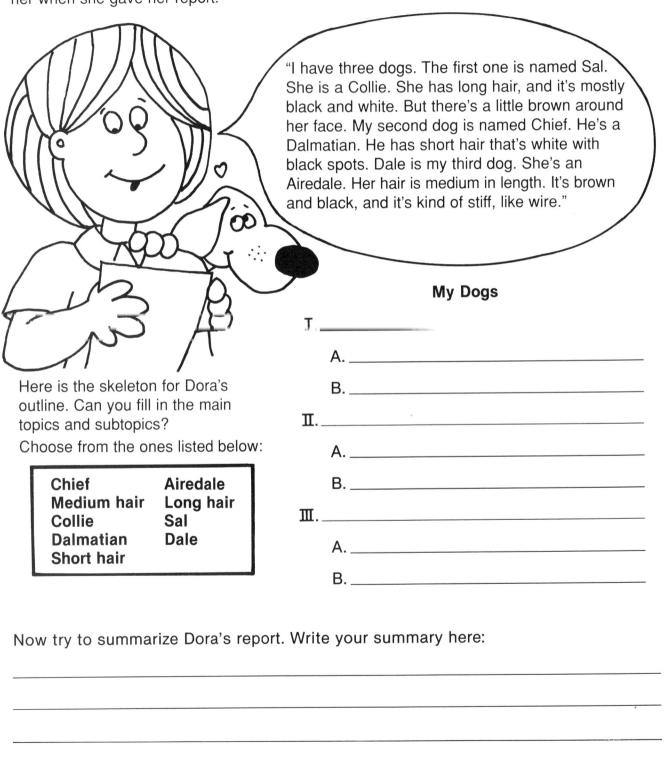

"I have three dogs. The first one is named Sal. She is a Collie. She has long hair, and it's mostly black and white. But there's a little brown around her face. My second dog is named Chief. He's a Dalmatian. He has short hair that's white with black spots. Dale is my third dog. She's an Airedale. Her hair is medium in length. It's brown and black, and it's kind of stiff, like wire."

My Dogs

I. _____

  A. _____

  B. _____

II. _____

  A. _____

  B. _____

III. _____

  A. _____

  B. _____

Here is the skeleton for Dora's outline. Can you fill in the main topics and subtopics?

Choose from the ones listed below:

Chief	**Airedale**
Medium hair	**Long hair**
Collie	**Sal**
Dalmatian	**Dale**
Short hair	

Now try to summarize Dora's report. Write your summary here:

_____

_____

_____

Name_____ Date _____

The Great Library Mystery

Finding a book in the library is no mystery if you know how the books are arranged. Fiction books are put on the shelves alphabetically by the author's last name. In most libraries nonfiction books are arranged numerically by their Dewey decimal number.

Every library book has letters or numbers known as the call number. You will find a call number on the spine of each library book. It is there to help you find the book on the shelf. Read the call number on each book below. Then draw a line from the book to its correct place on the shelf.

FICTION

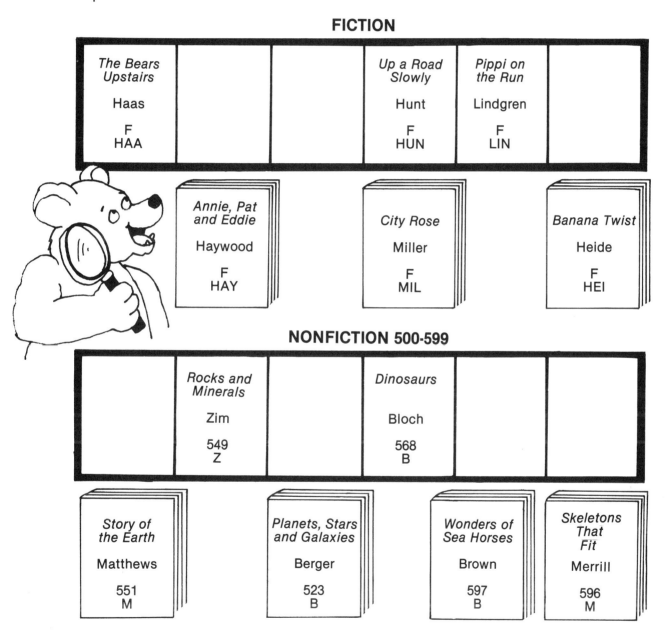

| The Bears Upstairs Haas F HAA | | | Up a Road Slowly Hunt F HUN | Pippi on the Run Lindgren F LIN | |

Annie, Pat and Eddie — Haywood — F HAY

City Rose — Miller — F MIL

Banana Twist — Heide — F HEI

NONFICTION 500-599

| | Rocks and Minerals Zim 549 Z | | Dinosaurs Bloch 568 B | | |

Story of the Earth — Matthews — 551 M

Planets, Stars and Galaxies — Berger — 523 B

Wonders of Sea Horses — Brown — 597 B

Skeletons That Fit — Merrill — 596 M

Name _____   Date _____

Paula's Puzzling Problem

In the Dewey decimal system, books are grouped into 10 main subject classes. Librarians assign a number to each book. The number is written on the book, and books with similar numbers are kept together.

Help!

The 10 main subject classes and their numbers are listed in the right-hand column below. In the left-hand column are the titles of ten new books. The librarian asked Paula what subject class each new book belonged in. Can you help solve Paula's puzzling problem? Draw a line from each title to the correct subject class.

Book Titles	Dewey Decimal Classifications	
1. A Complete History of the American Revolutionary War	000–099	General Works, such as encyclopedias
2. How a Television Works	100–199	Philosophy and Psychology
3. What's Wrong With Our Economy?	200–299	Religion
	300–399	Social Sciences, such as economics and law
4. Photography Made Simple		
5. Child Psychology for Parents	400–499	Language and grammar
6. Seventeenth Century Poetry	500–599	Science, such as astronomy and chemistry
7. Let's Look at the Stars in the Sky	600–699	Technology, such as television and engineering
8. Easy Grammar Tips for Everyone	700–799	Fine Arts, such as painting, photography, and sculpture
9. Religions of the Far East	800–899	Literature and Poetry
10. The All-Color Picture Encyclopedia	900–999	History and Geography

Name_____ Date _____

Library Crossword

What did the math book say to the reading book? To find out, use the clues to fill in the squares below. (The words in the box will help you.) Then read down the shaded squares to find the answer to the riddle.

1. An alphabetical list of names and subjects with the page numbers on which they appear in a book is called a(n) _____.

2. A special dictionary of words used in a book is called a(n) _____.

3. The name of a book is the _____.

4. The writer of a book is called a(n) _____.

5. The page of a book that tells the title, author, illustrator, publisher and place of publication is called the _____.

6. The _____ protects the pages of the book.

7. The main part of a book is called the _____.

8. A collection of extra information usually included at the end of a book is called a(n) _____.

9. The person who makes the pictures for a book is called a(n) _____.

10. A list of chapters and main sections of a book and the pages on which they begin is called the _____.

11. A list of books or articles about a specific subject is called the _____.

12. The person or company who prints a book is called the _____.

13. The _____ is an introductory section to a book. The author sometimes uses this section to describe what the book is going to be about.

14. The _____ is printed on the spine of a library book. It helps you find the book on the shelf.

15. The _____ of the book is the part you see when the book is on the shelf.

| appendix |
| glossary |
| spine |
| call number |
| preface |
| title |
| bibliography |
| index |
| author |
| illustrator |
| table of contents |
| cover |
| publisher |
| title page |
| text |

Name _____ Date _____

Clumsy Clarence

Clumsy Clarence did it again. On his way out of the library, he knocked over two bookshelves. Can you help put the books back? Read the title of each book. Decide whether the book is fiction or non-fiction. (Remember, fiction is a book that tells a made-up story. Nonfiction is a book that has facts and ideas about something that is real.) Then write the titles and authors on the appropriate lines. Be sure to arrange the fiction books alphabetically according to the author's last name.

Help!

Miss Pickerell Goes to Mars, Ellen MacGregor
How to Draw Cats, Janet Rancan
Last of the Dinosaurs, David Eastman
Adventures of Tom Sawyer, Mark Twain
The Invisible Man, by H.G. Wells
A Day in the Life of a Rock Musician, David Palge
Danny Dunn and the Homework Machine, Jay Williams
Animals That Use Tools, Barbara Ford
First Book of Presidents, Harold Coy
Spaceship in the Park, Louis Slobodkin
A Journey to the Center of the Earth, by Jules Verne
Soccer Tips, David Clements

FICTION   **NONFICTION**

_____   _____

_____   _____

_____   _____

_____   _____

_____   _____

_____   _____

Name_____   Date _____

Who's Who?

A *biography* is a book about a real person.
It is written by another person. An *autobiography* is
a book written by a person about his or her own life.

Below is a list of biographies and autobiographies. For each book, draw a line under
the name that tells who the book is about. Draw a circle around the name that tells
who wrote the book. Then, write **B** for biography, and **A** for autobiography
on the lines provided.

Helen Keller: The Story of My Life, Helen Keller   _____

Clara Barton: Angel of the Battlefield, Rae Bains   _____

My Diary, Edmund Zabriskie   _____

Sports Star: Tommy John, S. H. Burchard   _____

Ferdinand Magellan, Ruth Harley   _____

Sacajawea: Wilderness Guide, Kate Jassem   _____

Harriet Tubman: The Road to Freedom, Rae Bains   _____

Biographies and autobiographies are special kinds of
nonfiction. They are usually shelved together in one
section of the library. They are arranged in alphabetical
order according to the subject's last name. On the lines
below, rewrite the above titles in the order in which they
would be arranged in the library.

_____

_____

_____

_____

_____

_____

_____

Name_____ Date _____

47

For Your Information

Listed below are descriptions of the most frequently used sources of information found in libraries. Write the name of each source on the line below its description. Use the Word Bank if you need help.

1. This book tells you the spelling, pronunciation, and definition of words. The words are arranged alphabetically.

   _____

2. This book may be one book or a set of books. It contains general information on many subjects. The information is arranged alphabetically by topics.

   _____

3. This is a book of maps, graphs, and tables that gives geographic information.

   _____

4. Sometimes called a gazetteer, this book gives information about different places in the world. The names are arranged alphabetically.

   _____

5. This book, published yearly, contains current facts and statistics on a variety of subjects. Information is indexed by topics.

   _____

6. This book contains short biographies about famous people. The names are arranged alphabetically.

   _____

7. This is an index to articles that have been published in magazines.

8. This book lists synonyms (words with similar meanings) and antonyms (words with opposite meanings). The words are arranged in alphabetical order.

   _____

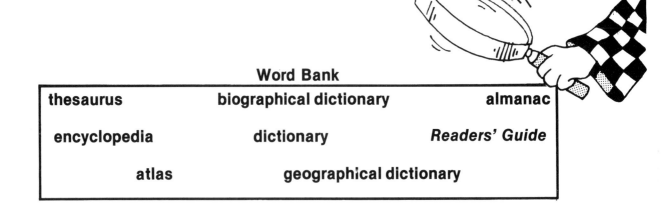

Word Bank

thesaurus	biographical dictionary	almanac
encyclopedia	dictionary	*Readers' Guide*
atlas	geographical dictionary	

Time to Talk

One of the best ways to gather information is to ask someone. People in your family or neighborhood have been witnesses to history.

In the last 50 years, the world has changed in many ways. The United States has been involved in several wars, from World War II to the Korean War to the wars in Vietnam and the Persian Gulf. Computers, unknown to most people 30 years ago, are now common, and rock and roll has spread all over the world. The Civil Rights movement, which began in the South, changed the way all Americans lived. Women struggled to become more independent and successful. The work people do has changed over the last half century, too.

Plan to interview someone you know about a historical event or trend. Once you have chosen your topic, prepare a list of questions. Some of the questions you ask could be about what the person did during the event. What does the person remember about the leaders of the time? How did the person feel about what was happening? Write your questions below.

_____

_____

_____

_____

_____

_____

_____

_____

Take notes while you are interviewing or use a cassette recorder. Transcribe your recording after your interview.

Combine the facts and stories you've heard into a report. Use the back of this sheet.

Name_____ **Date** _____

Research an Animal

1. Pick an animal you'd like to learn about.
   Then visit the library to find out the following:
   - How large does it grow?
   - Where did it develop?
   - What is the history of its development?
   - How is it used by people?

2. Look through encyclopedias and other reference books
   for general background information.

3. Look in the computer for the names of specific books
   you'll need.

4. Use the call numbers to help you find the books on the shelf.

5. Take notes on what you read to record the facts and ideas
   you want to remember.

6. In your own words, write an outline or a report that provides
   the answers for question #1 above.

On the lines below, record your sources of information. Write your report
on a separate piece of paper.

CALL NUMBER	TITLE	AUTHOR	PAGES USED

Name_____ Date _____

Extra! Extra!

Many libraries keep old copies of newspapers and magazines for months. After a while, they transfer newspapers to microfilm, which takes less space to store. You can read these old newspapers on a microfilm machine, which the librarian will show you how to use.

What was the top sports or local news story last Monday? To find out, consult your town or city newspaper published on that day. You will find it at the library. You could also call the editorial department of the newspaper and ask. Write the headline of the story.

_____

_____

What was happening on the international scene a year ago today? Ask the librarian to help you find out.

_____

_____

_____

_____

What was the weather report for the day you were born? The newspaper published on that day will tell you. What was the big sports story of that day? What movies and television shows were being shown then?

_____

_____

_____

_____

_____

What else was happening during the week or month of your birth? Check magazines or almanacs to find out.

_____

_____

_____

Name_____ **Date** _____

Check the Facts

Many magazines and publishers hire people to check the facts in articles and books. There are some errors in the paragraph below. Pretend you are a fact checker. Double-check each fact to make sure it is correct. Use the dictionary, encyclopedia, almanac, or any other helpful source.

> *Mountains cover about one third of the Earth's land. The Himalayan range, which includes some of the highest mountains in the world, extends over approximately 1,550 miles or 2,500 kilometers. Mt. Everest, in south-central Australia, is the highest mountain on Earth. Many people tried to climb Mt. Everest, but the first to reach the summit were Sir Edward Hillary of Ireland and Tenzing Norgay of Nepal. They made their famous climb in 1963.*

Did you find any errors? List them below.

_____

_____

_____

_____

_____

_____

_____

_____

_____

_____

Bring in a newspaper article and circle all the facts that can be checked. Then draw lines under those facts it would be much more difficult to check. Draw boxes around opinions or speculations, statements that can't be checked at all. Do all three types of statements belong in a newspaper? Why?

Name_____ **Date** _____

Letter to the Editor

People write letters to the editors of newspapers to express their opinions on important issues. These letters are printed on the opinion or editorial page.

Do you care deeply about a particular issue? Express your thoughts in a letter to the editor of your local newspaper. Before you begin to write, decide on your topic. In your opinion, is something wrong in your school or town? Do you have ideas on how to fix it? What about movies, television, or music? Does anything in those fields get you excited? How about sports or medicine or politics?

Once you have thought about different topics, choose one and state your opinion.
Write it here. _____

_____

Make a list of the reasons you hold your opinion. Write down why you feel the way you do.

1. _____

2. _____

3. _____

4. _____

5. _____

Write an opening sentence that clearly expresses your opinion.

_____

_____

_____

_____

Then, use the points you've listed above to convince the reader that you are right.
Use the back of this sheet for a draft of your letter. Address it to "Dear Editor."

Name_____ Date _____

How Do I Get There?

Study the map.

1. What if someone at the library asked you how to get to Maple Court?
    Could you give clear directions? Write them below.

    _____

    _____

    _____

2. A woman just got off the bus. How can she get to the library?

    _____

    _____

    _____

    _____

3. Jonathan lives on the corner of Tulip Street and Oak Avenue. How can he get to
    high school?

    _____

    _____

    _____

    _____

Name_____ **Date** _____

The Right Recipe

Recipes are directions for cooking or preparing foods. They have to be clear and easy to follow.

Choose a food you have prepared or watched someone else prepare. It can be a cooked food, like scrambled eggs or grilled-cheese sandwiches, or it can be an uncooked food, like peanut butter-and-jelly sandwiches.

List all the ingredients in the correct amounts needed to prepare your food.

_____

_____

_____

_____

List the necessary tools, such as knives or pots.

_____

_____

_____

_____

Write how to make your food, one step at a time. Number your steps.

_____

_____

_____

_____

_____

_____

_____

_____

Tell how many people your recipe will feed. _____

Bon Appetit!

Name_____ Date _____

Roving Reporter

A good reporter knows that the lead (first) paragraph of a news story gives the most important facts. It tries to answer these questions:

Who?	What?	When?
Where?	Why?	How?

Think about something that happened in your family, school, or neighborhood in the last few days. Write a news story based on that event.

1. Write an interesting headline.

_____

2. Write a lead paragraph. Try to answer these questions: Who are the main characters? What happened to them? When did it happen? Where did it happen? Why did it happen? How did it happen?

_____
_____
_____
_____
_____

3. Now write the rest of the story.

_____
_____
_____
_____
_____
_____
_____
_____
_____
_____
_____
_____
_____

Name_____ **Date** _____

Write an Ad

Pretend you work for an advertising agency, and you've just been asked to prepare a newspaper or magazine advertisement for a book. Choose a book you have enjoyed reading. Write a short summary, making the book sound as exciting as you can. Make up some critics' quotes, recommending the book. Add a few descriptive phrases, if you like.

Book Title: _____

Author: _____

Publisher: _____

Cost: _____

Headline: _____

Summary: _____

_____

_____

_____

Quotes: _____

_____

_____

_____

Descriptive Phrases: _____

_____

_____

_____

Now put all your material together and write and design your newspaper or magazine ad on the back of this sheet.

Keep in Touch

A typical friendly letter has five parts. You should include them when you write to a friend or relative.

1. The *heading* shows your address and the date you are writing.
2. The *greeting* is your way of saying "Hello."
3. The *body* tells the message—your reason for writing.
4. The *closing* is your way of saying "Goodbye."
5. The *signature* tells it was you who wrote the letter.

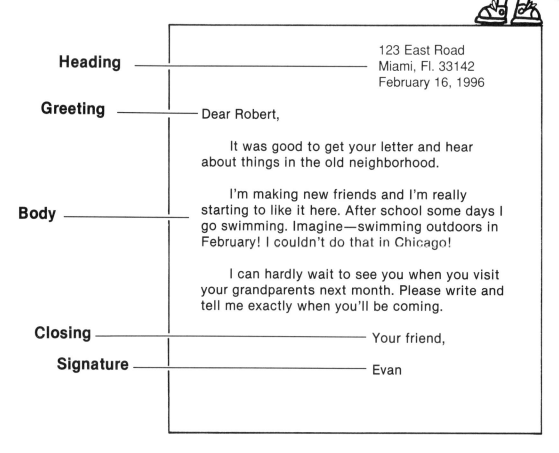

Heading — 123 East Road
Miami, Fl. 33142
February 16, 1996

Greeting — Dear Robert,

It was good to get your letter and hear about things in the old neighborhood.

Body — I'm making new friends and I'm really starting to like it here. After school some days I go swimming. Imagine—swimming outdoors in February! I couldn't do that in Chicago!

I can hardly wait to see you when you visit your grandparents next month. Please write and tell me exactly when you'll be coming.

Closing — Your friend,

Signature — Evan

On the back of this paper, write a letter to a friend or relative. Choose one of the following:

• Write to a friend who has moved away.
• Write to your parents (pretend you are away at summer camp).
• Write to your grandparents to thank them for the bike they gave you for your birthday.
• Write to invite someone to come to a party or to spend a weekend at your house.

Be sure to include all five parts in your letter. Use the sample letter as a guide.

Name_____ Date _____

Clearly Stated

A business letter has six parts.

1. The *heading* includes the writer's address and the date.

2. The *inside address* shows the name and address of the person or business to whom the letter is written.

3. The *salutation* greets the reader.

4. The *body* of the letter tells what the writer wants to say.

5. The *closing* says "goodbye." Some common closings: *Sincerely yours, Very truly yours.*

6. The *signature* tells who the writer is. If the letter is typed, the writer's name is typed below the signature. If the writer has a job title, it is typed below the name.

> 7777 Park Avenue
> New York, New York 10010
> June 18, 1993
>
> Ms. Sara Black
> 22 Ridge Road
> Fairmont, West Virginia 26554
>
> Dear Ms. Black:
>
> Thank you for your recent one-year subscription to *Teentime* Magazine. Your first issue should arrive within the next two weeks.
>
> Happy reading!
>
> Sincerely yours,
>
> *Lucy Rettle*
>
> Lucy Rettle
> Circulation Manager

Use the business letter above to answer these questions.

1. Who wrote the letter? _____

2. What is the writer's address? _____

3. When was the letter written? _____

4. To whom is the letter being sent, _____
   at what address? _____

5. What words were used as the closing? _____

6. Draw a circle around the salutation.

7. Draw a box around the body of the letter.

On the back of this paper, write your own business letter. Write to a real business or to one you've made up. Choose one of the following reasons to write:

• You want to order something by mail.
• You want to ask for information.
• You want to give information.
• You have a problem or a complaint.

Name_____ Date _____

In the Mail

Sheri Lane lives in apartment 5F, at 100 Lime Avenue, Fort Lee, New Jersey. Sheri's zip code is 07024. She wrote a letter to her friend, Wendy Gray, in Rochester, Minnesota. Wendy lives in a new house at 44 Chestnut Street. Her zip code is 55901. Sheri put the letter in the envelope below. Can you address it?

My favorite mailman.

Draw an envelope on the back of this paper. Address it to your local mayor or fire chief, or to your doctor or state senator. Use abbreviations wherever possible.

Name _____ Date _____

Apply Yourself

Did you ever enter a contest? Subscribe to a magazine? Apply to join a club?

If you did, chances are you've had to fill out an application or a questionnaire. When you fill out these forms, you must be sure to correctly fill in all the information that is asked for. Your writing must be neat and clear.

Fill out the order form below. Be sure to follow all the directions on the form.

To get your CRUNCHEE MUNCHEE TEE, just send $1.00 plus 2 boxtops from any size box of Crunchee Munchees for each shirt you want. Fill out the form below and mail to:

Crunchee Munchee Tee
878 Cereal Boulevard
Oshkosh, WI 54901

PLEASE PRINT

Please send _____ Crunchee Munchee Tees. For each shirt I am enclosing $5.00 plus two boxtops.

Name _____
         (First)   (Middle)   (Last)

Mailing Address _____
              (Number & Street)   (City)   (State)   (Zip Code)

Quantity   Size (Check One)

_____   ____Small   ____Medium   ____Large

_____   ____Small   ____Medium   ____Large

_____   ____Small   ____Medium   ____Large

Total Amount Enclosed $_____   Total Number of Boxtops _____

Your Signature (Do not print) _____

On the back of this paper, draw an envelope. Address it as if you were going to mail the above coupon.

Name_____   Date _____

Let's Go to the Movies

It's a rainy Saturday and you've decided to go to the movies. What will you see? And at what time? To help you decide, you need to know how to read a movie schedule. It tells the name of the movie playing at each theater and the times each movie is shown. Read the movie schedule to answer the questions below.

THE MOVIES					
Cinema 1 *Daredevil Dogs* [G]	2:00	4:00	6:00	8:00	10:00
Cinema 2 *Moe & Joe* [G]	2:15	4:00	5.45	7.30	9.15
Cinema 3 *Marvelous Monsters* [PG]	2:30	5:30	8:30		

1. What theater is showing *Marvelous Monsters*?_____

2. How many times a day is *Daredevil Dogs* shown? _____

3. At what time is the first showing of *Moe & Joe*? _____

    At what time is the last showing of *Moe & Joe*? _____

4. What time does the first show of *Marvelous Monsters* begin? _____

    What time does the next show of *Marvelous Monsters* begin?_____

    About how long does the movie last? _____

5. Why are there fewer showings of *Marvelous Monsters* than of *Daredevil Dogs* and *Moe & Joe*? _____

6. If you go to the 10:00 show of *Daredevil Dogs*, at what time will you probably be out of the theater? _____

7. Suppose you get to the theater at 5 P.M. You don't want to see a movie that has already started. You want to spend as little time as possible waiting. Which movie will you see? _____

Using a movie schedule clipped from your local newspaper, make up questions about the schedule and give them to a friend to answer.

Name_____ Date _____

Super Skates

The schedule on this page gives information about different sessions at
Super Skates Roller Rink. Use the schedule to answer these questions.

1. On what day is the roller rink closed? _____

2. On what days are lessons given? _____

3. If you are in Intermediate Class 2, when do you take your skating lessons?
   _____

4. You are planning a private skating party for your birthday. On what days
   and at what times could you have your party? _____

5. What kind of skating can you do at 9:00 P.M. on a Thursday? _____

6. At what time does the roller rink open on Wednesdays? _____

7. How many days a week is there a Roller Disco session? _____

8. It's 6:00 on a Friday night. You and your family want to go roller skating.
   Can you? _____

SUPER SKATES							
Time	**Monday**	**Tuesday**	**Wednesday**	**Thursday**	**Friday**	**Saturday**	**Sunday**
A.M. 9:00–11:30	CLOSED	CLOSED	CLOSED	CLOSED	CLOSED	LESSONS Beg. 1 Int. I Adv. 1	LESSONS Beg. 2 Int. 2 Adv. 2
P.M. 12:00–3:00	CLOSED	CLOSED	CLOSED	CLOSED	CLOSED	General Admission	General Admission
4:00–6:00	CLOSED	Reserved for Private Groups	General Admission	Reserved for Private Groups	General Admission	General Admission	General Admission
6:00–8:00	CLOSED	General Admission	LESSONS Beg. 3 Int. 3 Adv. 3	General Admission	General Admission	General Admission	General Admission
8:00–10:00	CLOSED	General Admission	General Admission	Roller Disco	Roller Disco	Roller Disco	General Admission

Name_____ Date _____

The Great Getaway

If you want to travel by train, bus, or airplane, you'll need to know how to read a timetable. **A timetable gives the schedule that the train, bus, or plane follows.** It tells:

- departure and arrival
- cities (towns) you can travel to
- days of the week you can travel

Use the train timetable on this page to answer the questions below:

1. I just missed the 2:30 P.M. train from Danbury to New York. What time is the next train I can take?

2. Does the 6:40 A.M. train from Danbury stop in Reddington?

3. On weekends and holidays, what time does the last train leave Reddington for New York?

4. How long is the trip from Danbury to New York?

5. I need to be in New York by 9:00 A.M. on Friday. What is the latest train I can take from Wilton?

6. What time does the 8:00 P.M. weekday train from Danbury stop in South Norwalk?

DANBURY — NEW YORK				
(light type = A.M. dark type = P.M.)				
Monday through Friday, except holidays				
LEAVE				ARRIVE
Danbury	Reddington	Wilton	S. Norwalk	New York
6:00	6:15	6:35	6:55	7:55
6:40	.....	7:15	.....	8:35
7:20	7:35	7:55	8:15	9:15
10:30	10:45	11:05	11:25	**12:25**
2:30	**2:45**	**3:05**	**3:25**	**4:25**
5:00	**5:15**	**5:35**	**5:55**	**6:55**
8:00	**8:15**	**8:35**	**8:55**	**9:55**
Weekends and Holidays				
7:00	7:15	7:35	7:55	8:55
11:00	11:15	11:35	11:55	**12:55**
3:00	**3:15**	**3:35**	**3:55**	**4:55**
7:00	**7:15**	**7:35**	**7:55**	**8:55**

How many different kinds of tables or schedules can you collect?

Find It Fast

The White Pages of the telephone book list names of people and businesses in alphabetical order. Two guide words at the top of each page show the first and last name on the page. To find a telephone number quickly:

- Use the guide words to help you find the right page.
- Look across the page to find the column the name will be in.
- Look down the column to find the name.

Draw a line to match each pair of guide words with the name you'd find on that page.	Draw a line to show in which column you would find each name.
Guide Words *Listing*	*Field* *Finn*
Landry-Lang Bradford	Figaro
Keegan-Kessler Lipton	Fipps
Boyd-Brady Klaus	Fine
Lindsay-Lisbon Keller	Fimmel
King-Kramer Lane	

Here are some hints to help you find telephone numbers quickly.

- Names are listed in alphabetical order with the last name first.
- When last names are the same, the names are listed alphabetically by first names.
- Initials are listed before names.
- Abbreviations are listed alphabetically as if the names were spelled out.
- Numbers in names are listed as if they were spelled out.

SAMPLE

156 Saint A - Sparks

St. Ann's School 43 Flower . . . .
71 St. Garage 11W71St . . . .
Smith, H 25W10St . . . .
Smith, Helen 11 Marcus . . . .
Smith, Irene 100 West . . . .

Rewrite the following names and list them in the order in which they would appear in the phone book.

John Stiles   James Morgan   16th Street Drug Store   J. Stiles
Ramon Suarez   J.R. Stiles   Mt. Pleasant Ski Shop   Maria Suarez

1. _____

2. _____

3. _____

4. _____

5. _____

6. _____

7. _____

8. _____

Name_____   Date _____

Goods & Services

The Yellow Pages lists companies under headings that describe their business or service. The headings are listed in alphabetical order, and so are the names under each heading. Guide words at the top of each page indicate the first and last heading on the page.

Draw a line to match each business or individual with the heading under which it would be listed in the Yellow Pages. Then draw a line from each heading to the guide words under which it would appear.

BUSINESS	HEADING	GUIDE WORDS
Pete's Pizzas	Pharmacies	Delivery - Dentists
The Hobby House	Lawyers	Paving - Pewter
Puppy Palace	Toys-Retail	Lawn - Lawyers
Ray Cook, Atty.	Dentists	Pharmacies - Photo
Bergen Drugs	Pet Shops	Restaurants - Restaurants
Martha Chang, DDS.	Restaurants	Towing - Trailers

How would the following businesses be listed in the Yellow Pages?
Put them in the order in which they would appear under the right heading.

Super Scissors   Music Madness   East Side Haircutters
Ken's Barber Shop   Steve's Stereo Shop   Dynamite Discs
Kool Cuts   House of Hair   Stereo Surprise
Record World

BARBERS   RECORDS, TAPES & COMPACT DISCS

_____   _____

_____   _____

_____   _____

_____   _____

_____   _____

*Suppose you want to buy a new bike. Where will you go?
 Check in your local Yellow Pages to answer these questions.

1. Under what heading will you look? _____

2. How many listings are under that heading? _____

3. What are the guide words? _____

4. Write the names of two listings and tell why you might go to one store instead of the other.

_____

_____

Name_____   Date _____

Shopping Shortcuts

Not all listings in the Yellow Pages look alike. Many businesses place advertisements along with their listings. Use the listings below to answer the questions.

At which rink can you

1. ice skate and roller skate?

_____

2. play hockey? _____

3. take your 4-year old cousin for skating lessons?

_____

Which rink

4. rents roller skates?

_____

5. is closed most weekday afternoons?

_____

6. has a snack bar? _____

7. does not have an ad?

_____

8. has special prices for groups?

_____

9. What number would you call to find out the hours Roll-A-Round is open?

_____

10. Where would you look for more information about Whacky Wheels?

_____

SIGNS-SKATING	321

SKATING RINKS

ICE WORLD
25BwyArmt 121-2211
(See Advertisement This Page)

MAGIC ROLLER RINK
Evenings: 7-11
Sat Sun & School Hol: 2-5
    GROUP RATES * RENTALS
Route 1 & Hghlnd Redburg
(Across from Magic Mall) 343-1133

ROLL-A-ROUND
20EMainWstvle 323-1132

SKATE LAND
Both Ice & Roller Skating
23 RockRdBlmg 788-1133

SKATE WORLD
11 GraceAvHghpk 429-3322
(See Advertisement This Page)

WHACKY WHEELS
199ParkPlArmt 121-4565
(See Advertisement Page 322)

ICE WORLD

Open Year Round   *   7 Days a Week
Pro Shop   Snack Bar   Rentals
    Hockey   Public Skating

121-2211   25 Broadway   Airmont

SKATE WORLD
Indoor Ice Skating at its Best

Open Year Round

Public Skating   Lessons
    Tiny Tots Program Ages 3-5
11 Grace Avenue   Highpark

429-3322

Emergency! Emergency!

Help! Help! Imagine that your neighbors are away on vacation and you see smoke coming out of their house. What do you do? In an emergency, the fastest way to get help is to dial the number yourself—in this case, the number of the fire department. If you don't know it, dial 911 or "O" (Operator) for help. The most important thing to say first is, "THIS IS AN EMERGENCY."

Then say:

- what the emergency is.
- your name.
- the telephone number you are calling from.
- the address where help is needed.

This is an EMERGENCY!

If possible, don't hang up right away. The dispatcher may need more information or may have information to give you.

Will you know what to do in an emergency? Pretend you are at home taking care of your four-year-old brother. He falls and cuts his knees. Who would you call? What would you say?

_____

_____

_____

In most communities, emergency numbers are listed in the front of the telephone book. Check in your telephone book and write each of the numbers someone would need to report an emergency from your house. Include your own telephone number and address, too. Then cut out the list and put it near the telephone in your house. If you have more than one phone, make a copy of the list. Put one copy near each phone.

EMERGENCY TELEPHONE NUMBERS

FIRE _____   POLICE _____

AMBULANCE _____   POISON CONTROL _____

Doctor _____   Gas _____   Electric _____

This Number _____   This Address _____

_____

Name_____   Date _____

It's for You!

Be polite and helpful when you answer the phone. If the call is not for you, offer to take a message. Always write down the name of the person calling.

Read the questions. Choose the best response and circle it.

1. "Is your mother home?" (She isn't.)
   a. "If you tell me your name, she'll call you back as soon as she can."
   b. "I don't know. I don't see her."
   c. "How should I know?"

2. "I want to talk to Rebecca right away. Why doesn't she ever call me back?"
   a. "Hold on. I'll see if she's here."
   b. "Don't ask me. I'm not a mindreader."
   c. "Rebecca who?"

3. "This is Zarakh Smorzynski. Is your father home?" (He isn't.)
   a. "Who is this?"
   b. "If you spell your name, I'll write it down and tell him you called."
   c. "Is that your real name?"

Although you should always be polite, you do not need to offer information.

4. "When will your parents be home? It's important that I talk to them."
   a. "I don't know. Good-bye."
   b. "I'm not supposed to talk to strangers."
   c. "I can write your name and phone number down and give it to them."

5. "I'm sure your mother will want to order this magazine. Why don't you give me her office number?"
   a. "She can call you if she's interested. What is your phone number?"
   b. "Okay, it's 479–8341."
   c. "She works at City Hospital. Look it up."

Name_____ Date _____

Eating Out

PITA PALACE

SANDWICHES**

Chicken Salad	.3.00
Egg Salad	.2.85
Grilled Cheese	.2.65
Peanut Butter 'N Jelly	.2.50
Tuna Salad	.3.00

**All sandwiches served on our
  freshly-baked pita bread.

* Tomato slices 20¢ extra.

SPECIALS

Burger	.2.75
With Cheese	.2.95
Pizza	.3.00

SOUPS AND SALADS

Soup of the Day	.1.60
Cole Slaw	.1.35
Tossed Salad	.1.50
Spinach Salad	.1.50

BEVERAGES

Milk	.1.40
Fruit Juices	.1.45
Yogurt Shake	.1.65
Tea: Hot	.75
Cold	.95
Coffee	.75

DESSERTS

Yogurt Cone	.1.55
Yogurt Sundae	.1.95
Carob Crunch Cookies	.1.45
Fresh Fruit	.1.50

ALL ITEMS ON THE MENU MAY BE ORDERED TO TAKE HOME

Imagine you are having lunch at the Palace. Use the menu to answer the following questions.

1. What would you order from the menu?
   How much does it cost? _____

2. How much is charged for adding cheese to a burger? _____

3. What is the cost of a tuna-salad sandwich with tomato? _____

4. Is take-out service available? _____ Does it cost extra? _____

5. How much more does a yogurt sundae cost than a yogurt cone? _____

6. What is the least expensive sandwich on the menu? _____

7. Which of the following lunches can you buy for less than $6.00?

Lunch 1	**Lunch 2**	**Lunch 3**
Chicken-Salad Sandwich	Burger	Grilled Cheese/tomato
Soup	Fruit Juice	Cole Slaw
Fresh Fruit	Yogurt Cone	Iced Tea
		Cookies

8. Suppose you order a tuna-salad sandwich and milk. Your friend orders a pizza and yogurt shake. Whose lunch costs more? _____ How much more? _____

The next time your family eats in a restaurant, ask if you can take home a copy of the menu. Use it to figure out the cost of different meals you might have.

Name_____ **Date** _____

The Best Source

Almanac	Atlas	Dictionary
Telephone Directory	Thesaurus	Encyclopedia

It's not important to know the answer to every question. But it is important to know how to find the answer. Each of the reference sources named above contains different kinds of information. When you have a question you want answered, you need to know which book is the best source—the one most likely to have the information you want.

Juan is looking for answers to the questions below. Next to each question write the name of the book he should look in first.

1. What happens to food after we eat it? _____

2. What is the meaning of the word *foreign*? _____

3. What countries border on the Mediterranean Sea? _____

4. When was Martin Luther King, Jr. born? _____

5. How do you pronounce *cache*? _____

6. What is another word for *destroy*? _____

7. How many syllables are in *serenade*? _____

8. What team won last year's Super Bowl? _____

9. Where can I read the highlights on Susan B. Anthony's life? _____

10. What road would you travel from San Francisco, CA, to Yosemite

    National Park? _____

11. What is the current population of your state? _____

12. How do fish breathe? _____

13. Where is there a river named *Lot*? _____

14. What is the telephone number of the nearest Poison Control Center?

    _____

Name_____ **Date** _____

Take a Trip

Imagine that you and your family can take a one-week trip anywhere in the United States. Decide where you'd like to go. Then get ready to plan your trip!

- Go to the library for background information about the place you want to visit.
- Contact an airline, train or bus company, or motor club for travel information and/or schedules.
- Write business letters to the Tourist Bureau or Chamber of Commerce of the place you want to visit for information about hotel/motel accommodations, weather conditions, and tourist information.

Use this page to keep a record of your research. You might even staple it to the inside of a folder and include information such as schedules, maps, and pamphlets you receive. Have a good trip!

1. Books and magazine articles I read. _____

_____

_____

_____

2. People or places I wrote to. _____

_____

_____

3. People or places I called. _____

_____

_____

_____

4. Travel information. How can I get there? How long will it take? How much will it cost?

_____

_____

_____

_____

Name_____ Date _____

Sound Off!

Many people write to their representatives in Congress to express their opinions on the issues of the day. You can do the same. First, find out the name and address of your United States representative and senator.

Senator   Congressman or Congresswoman

_____ | _____

_____ | _____

_____ | _____

_____ | _____

Now, choose an issue that you care about. It might concern education, crime, communications, medicine, or the environment. Write down some points you wish to make.

_____

_____

_____

_____

_____

You are ready to write your letter. Organize the points you made above and write a first draft of a business letter on the back of this sheet. Revise, and write the final copy on a clean sheet of paper. Address an envelope and mail your letter, if you wish. By doing so, you are taking part in the democratic process. You may even get a reply!

Name_____   **Date** _____

Believe It or Not

Use reference books and double-check the following amazing facts to see if they are true or false. Then write T or F on the line. If the sentence is incorrect, write the correct fact.

1. Chickens lay fewer eggs in Alaska than any other state. _____

_____

2. "Sesame Street" has been on television for 15 years. _____

_____

3. The average teacher's annual salary in 1900 was $325.00. _____

_____

4. When a United States flag is torn or tattered, it should be destroyed by burning.

_____

_____

5. During one day in 1924, 22 tornadoes caused over $10 million of damage in the
   South and Midwest. ___   _____

   _____   _____

6. The Red Death, which swept through Europe from 1347 to 1351, killed approximately
   75 million people. _____

   _____

7. The first comic strip appeared in 1897. _____

   _____

8. The first manned spaceflight to take more than 24 hours took place 25 years ago.

   _____

   _____

9. At the first intercollegiate football game, which was played in Pennsylvania, players
   were not allowed to run with the ball. _____

   _____

10. Historians believe Western outlaw Billy the Kid was born in New York City.

    _____

    _____